Making Peace with Your Father

Other Works by Al Hill

Our Evil—God's Good
And Other Sermons from Genesis through Joshua

Things That Kings Can't Do
And Other Sermons from Judges through 2nd Kings, and the Wisdom Books

In the Presence of the Lord
And Other Sermons from the Psalms and the Prophets

Walking with Jesus
And Other Sermons from the Gospel of Matthew

God's Purpose for Your Faith
And Other Sermons from the Gospel of Mark, Hebrews, James and 1st Peter

From Jerusalem to Jericho
And Other Sermons from the Gospel of Luke and the Acts of the Apostles

Traits of the Shepherd
And Other Sermons from the Gospel of John, 1st John and Revelation

The Empty God
And Other Sermons from the Shorter Letters of Paul

O Come, Let God Adore Us
And Other Sermons for Advent and Christmas

Not Exactly What They Expected
And Other Sermons for Holy Week and Easter

DEAR TRINITY
Letters from a Pastor to His People

Making Peace with Your Father

*And Other Sermons from Paul's Letters
to the Romans and Corinthians*

Al Hill

SOMMERTON
HOUSE

ISBN: 978-1-948773-18-8 (sc)

Library of Congress Control Number: 2018944366

To learn more about, or to purchase, this or other works by Al Hill,

go to www.sommertonhouse.com

or www.amazon.com/author/alhill.

Dedication

To the memory of my father,
A. C. "Apie" Hill,

who did the best he could—
and better than most—
with the hard hand life dealt him.

More a prodigal son returned
than a natural saint,
he loved his own children fiercely,
and was always ready
to "kill the fatted calf" and celebrate
whenever his often-absent son
came home.

Contents

From the First Letter to the Corinthians

From the Second Letter to the Corinthians

Indices

Preface

Before the New Testament was formed, or the four Gospels were written, people like the Apostle Paul were taking the testimony of eye witnesses about Jesus—and their own experiences with the Risen Lord—to cities throughout the Roman Empire, making more disciples of Christ, as He had instructed them to do. Along the way, Paul composed letters of encouragement and instruction for the new converts he had left behind as he moved on to new places. The letters of 1st and 2nd Corinthians are two examples of Paul's efforts to explain and apply the gospel of the Jewish Messiah Who had become the Savior of the world—for Jews and Gentiles alike.

Paul's letter to the Romans is different from his other letters in that he directed it to a Christian congregation he had never met. Romans is Paul's letter of introduction to the believers in the imperial capital he hoped to visit (and eventually did). It is his longest letter and the most substantial in laying out, in a systematic way, his understanding of what the life, death and resurrection of Jesus Christ mean for humanity—and all Creation.

The Apostle Paul wrote the Roman church that *"since we are justified by faith, we have peace with God through our Lord Jesus Christ."*[1] This verse was the inspiration for the sermon that provides the title for this collection of sermons from Romans and the Corinthian

---

[1] Romans 6:1, RSV.

ix

letters. Though the title talks about "Making Peace with Your Father," comparing (and contrasting) our relationships with our earthly fathers to what we experience with our Heavenly Father, the truth is that the idea of "making peace with our Heavenly Father" is a misnomer. It is our Heavenly Father Who has been making peace with us.

In fact, the relationship between *"the God and Father of us all"*[2] and "all His children"—from Adam and Eve down to you and me—has always been problematic, even if we did not realize the relationship was in need of God's peace-making efforts—or we did not think any serious reconciliation with our Heavenly Father was possible.

Paul came to understand that all the problems we want to "fix" in our human, earthly existence require our attention, first, to our relationship with the One Who brought us all into being and sustains us every day. And in the pages of these first (in biblical order) and longest three letters of Paul, the Apostle digs deep into the meaning of the revelation of our Heavenly Father's love and grace and redemption and peace in Jesus Christ. The purpose of these sermons was—and is—to dig into what Paul discovered and see how we may apply what he found to our own needs today. Paul says we *"have peace"* with our Heavenly Father. The question is: Will we recognize it and claim it and embrace it for ourselves?

আ•৬

A few comments about the practical matters of this book may be helpful, and appropriate at this point. All the sermons here were written, in full, prior to being preached. They were, thus, written to be spoken out loud to a large group of people gathered in a sanctuary for worship. They were not written to be read by

---

[2] Ephesians 4:6, RSV.

individuals in whatever private setting and location they (you) may have chosen. This is why some sentences may seem to go on forever—and some don't seem to go on long enough to be classified as "complete." It's why you will encounter an inordinate amount of "em-dashes."

As a reader, you are at the disadvantage of not being able to "hear" the tone and inflection I applied to words and phrases. You cannot see the facial expressions, body language and physical gestures that accompanied the words in presentation. You will not be aware of all the contextual understandings I shared with the congregations in the various places these sermons were preached.

On the other hand, you will not have to mentally "screen out" the sounds of babies crying or cell phones ringing just as an important idea is being expressed. You can re-read anything that doesn't make sense the first time. You can go back and look at the scripture to clarify an allusion that may seem (and probably is) obscure. You can take up any sermon in the book at any time you want, rather than being stuck with whatever sermon I decided to preach on any given Sunday. And you can stick your book mark in the middle of a sermon and go do something else for a while. All these benefits were not available to the original audience.

&-&

Throughout the book, you will find that pronouns and other words referring to Father, Son or Holy Ghost have been capitalized, though this is no longer the general convention. The exception is in copyrighted translations of the Bible.

The footnotes are a later addition; I generally did not identify particular biblical passages as I preached, or give background information about music, media or historical events as I have done here. In scriptural references, a version is identified in the footnotes when phrases, verses or longer passages are actually quoted. When the scripture has been paraphrased, no version is indicated. The same is true for references whose purpose is to provide biblical support for some affirmation or allusion.

The sermon texts come from different versions of the Bible. The text used for each sermon reflects the version available to the congregation of the particular chapel and church where the sermon was preached. One version I used is no longer available for publication. In its place, I have substituted the *English Standard Version*.

To assist preachers and others who might want to maneuver more readily around the material, I have provided a set of indices in the back. All the footnoted scripture references throughout the book are listed in biblical order at the end. A list of Revised Common Lectionary connections is provided, as are an alphabetized list of sermon titles and a list of sermon texts in biblical order. And because sermons from Romans and 1ˢᵗ and 2ⁿᵈ Corinthians appear (or will) in what will eventually be 10 other volumes, I have indicated where they may be found in those books.

కిరిస్

I wrote these sermons because I was called to do so, to speak God's word to God's people under my pastoral care. The sermons probably spoke more to me than to anyone who heard them because I spent a great deal more time grappling with the words and ideas and insights that eventually became these sermons. I believe the hours spent in prayer and preparation were not spent alone, but in the presence—and under the direction—of the Holy Spirit. I pray that, as you read and consider, you will sense that you are not alone, either.

కిరిస్

Sermons

From the Letter to the Romans

Romans 1:8-16 ESV

[8] First, I thank my God through Jesus Christ for all of you, because your faith is proclaimed in all the world. [9] For God is my witness, whom I serve with my spirit in the gospel of his Son, that without ceasing I mention you [10] always in my prayers, asking that somehow by God's will I may now at last succeed in coming to you. [11] For I long to see you, that I may impart to you some spiritual gift to strengthen you— [12] that is, that we may be mutually encouraged by each other's faith, both yours and mine. [13] I do not want you to be unaware, brothers, that I have often intended to come to you (but thus far have been prevented), in order that I may reap some harvest among you as well as among the rest of the Gentiles. [14] I am under obligation both to Greeks and to barbarians, both to the wise and to the foolish. [15] So I am eager to preach the gospel to you also who are in Rome.

[16] For I am not ashamed of the gospel, for it is the power of God for salvation to everyone who believes, to the Jew first and also to the Greek.

തൻ

1.

Parties of the Second Part

Romans 1:8-16 ESV

Each Sunday, we read passages from the Bible, usually from a Gospel and a letter of Paul. We read what Jesus said and did two thousand years ago, and things Paul wrote to people who believed in Jesus and formed the first churches. It's all packaged up neatly for us within the covers of a book.

For that reason, we tend to approach the Bible as "third parties," observing the actions of other people and overhearing what Jesus or Paul has said to somebody else.

But suppose, in verse 7 of Romans 1, where it reads, *"To all God's beloved in Rome, who are called to be saints,"* a divine Hand had erased the word "Rome" and written in "Pinehurst," or even "The Village Chapel."[3] Suppose the title of the book were "The Letter of Paul to the Chapelians," or whatever the proper term is.

What happens when you read the Bible not as a "party of the third part," but of "the second"? What difference would it make if Paul were writing to *you*?

Is that far-fetched?

---

[3] This sermon was preached at The Village Chapel, an interdenominational church in Pinehurst, North Carolina.

Listen: *"I thank my God through Jesus Christ for all of you*—at The Village Chapel—*because your faith is proclaimed throughout the world."*

Does the idea of our faith being talked about around the world seem silly and presumptuous?

Well consider: We're supporting missionaries in Mongolia and Africa, the former Soviet Union and Spain. We're supporting mission work in Haiti and other areas of need. Don't you think they're telling people about your generosity in support of their work?

I don't have any trouble believing that the Apostle Paul knows who we are and prays to God for us all the time. He is in heaven with God. And since his arrival there, Paul has enjoyed all the knowledge he expected the saints in heaven to enjoy.[4] He is fully capable now of caring about you and me the way he cared about the Roman Christians during his life on earth.

But how do you make the case for Paul wanting to come to us and see us so that he *"can share some spiritual gift with"* us?

If the Apostle Paul were to show up here today in the flesh, I would probably be among the first to pass out.

But does that mean that Paul can't "come to us"—can't be thankful for our faith and want to do something or say something that will strengthen our faith? How could it be possible for Paul and the members of The Village Chapel to be *"mutually encouraged by each other's faith"*?

Let me suggest to you that Paul and John and Peter and Jesus Himself come to you when you hear their words. Don't your relationships with loved ones come to life—no matter how far away they are—when you read letters or emails from them? And when you hear from someone you know and love, and you know they are talking to you, you are a "party of the second part." What they say is for *you*; what they say "brings" them to you.

---

[4] 1 Corinthians 13:9-12.

Paul says, *"I have often intended to come to you (but thus far have been prevented)."*

Do you realize that all the giants of faith want to come to you—Abraham and Moses and David and the prophets and those I mentioned earlier—they all intend to come to you and strengthen you, just like Paul did with the Romans, but they have been prevented, thus far, from doing so?

What would prevent the giants of the faith from coming and strengthening the members of The Village Chapel?

If you do not read their words—if you do not allow them to speak to you—they cannot come to you as they intend.

You prevent them.

ॐ

"They read the Bible when I come to church."

And is once a week (assuming you never miss a service) how often you want Jesus and His disciples to come to you and strengthen you?

Don't shortchange yourself. Don't depend on someone else. Read the Bible yourself. Read the Bible every day. Read or listen to it throughout the day. Don't prevent these great saints—or the very Savior Himself—from coming to you as they intend.

"But I don't understand the Bible."

Then read it again. Read it longer and more often. Read it with others. Ponder it and pray over what you read.

If you meet a stranger and then spend a lot of time with him, pretty soon he will become a familiar friend. You'll get to know him. You will eagerly anticipate and cherish his visits. You will be blessed by his presence with you and what he has to say to you.

Read the Word. Paul and the others want to come to you and strengthen you. It's what they intend to do. God isn't preventing them—and you shouldn't, either.

ॐ

Romans 3:21-26 NRSV

[21] *But now, apart from law, the righteousness of God has been disclosed, and is attested by the law and the prophets,* [22] *the righteousness of God through faith in Jesus Christ for all who believe. For there is no distinction,* [23] *since all have sinned and fall short of the glory of God;* [24] *they are now justified by his grace as a gift, through the redemption that is in Christ Jesus,* [25] *whom God put forward as a sacrifice of atonement by his blood, effective through faith. He did this to show his righteousness, because in his divine forbearance he had passed over the sins previously committed;* [26] *it was to prove at the present time that he himself is righteous and that he justifies the one who has faith in Jesus.*

৯৯৯

2.

The God Who Won by the Rules

Romans 3:21-26 NRSV

Today, I feel a bit like I did the day my Dad took the training wheels off my bicycle and shoved me off on my own.[5] I was a bit wobbly, and thought for sure I was going to fall on my face any minute. But I eventually got the hang of it. And, with your patient indulgence, I'm sure I will here as well.

That said, let's move on to more important things—God things. Nothing is more important than what Paul is talking about in Romans, Chapter 3.

But sometimes—and especially in Romans—Paul makes the gospel sound like chemistry or physics or some kind of higher math. He gets to talking about righteousness and justification, then brings in redemption and expiation (or propitiation, depending on your translation) and rounds it off with something called "divine forbearance." If there's good news there, you're not going to know it unless you can translate it into some kind of language you understand.

---

[5] A few weeks after I joined the staff of a new church and began preaching and leading worship, the other minister with whom I would be sharing these duties left for a month's vacation.

Most people have an easier time with the language of sports, so let me draw in some sports terminology and concepts to bring Paul's points into sharper focus.

Success in sports calls for a certain level of skill. Different sports call for different skills, but all require a sufficient ability in the skills specific to that game. You may not need skills that are crucial to other sports. Your ability to dunk a basketball will not be of any benefit in hockey. Blazing speed is irrelevant on the golf course. The question is, "How well do you do what the game calls for?"

But games are not just about ability. Games have rules. The rules are what determine what game you're playing. You don't "kick a touchdown," as a former soccer star drafted by the NFL claimed to have done.[6] Apparently, according to a Tom Hanks movie character, "There's no crying in baseball."[7] There are rules.

Now there are a lot of very talented athletes who are failures because they cannot or will not obey the rules of their game. And, of course, there are many who abide by the rules but lose because they cannot do well enough what's required to win.

So keep these concepts in mind: sufficient skill to dominate the game and faithfulness to the rules that define the game. Now back to Paul's point in Romans 3.

⤎⊶⊷

Paul is talking about THE game—the ultimate game. And here I do not refer to golf—even to tournament play.[8] Paul is talking about "The Game of Life"—the contest that spans the breadth of time and space and all Creation. This is about the future of the world and every person in it. It's about how to get people out of

---

[6] Garo Yepremian, playing for the Detroit Lions during his rookie season in 1966.

[7] Tom Hanks played team manager Jimmy Dugan in *A League of Their Own*, 1992.

[8] This sermon was preached at The Village Chapel in Pinehurst, North Carolina, "The Birthplace of American Golf."

the trap of sin who do not have the ability to swing a club or even tee up the ball, morally speaking.

Of course, God can do what's needed. God can do anything—He's God. But God, in inventing "The Game of Life," also invented the rules that make the game playable. And it looks as though the only way God can win the game—can bring His divine, and certainly adequate, ability to save people from the death and destruction their sin has earned them (according to the rules of the game)—is to ignore the rules He established for the proper play of it.

But if He breaks the rules to win the game, God disqualified Himself in the process from being a righteous God. Righteousness is basically playing by the rules of the game—even when you have the ability to do otherwise.

જ⊶ઉ

But Paul says that God has won the game of restoring Creation and people to right relationship with Himself by giving Jesus Christ as the sacrifice for our sin. The death of Jesus Christ on the Cross was both the demonstration of God's ability to play the game successfully and the proof that He could and did protect us from the penalty we deserved for breaking the rules of life—without breaking those rules Himself.

He demonstrated His ability by defeating death for us and He restored us to the relationship with Himself He intended from the beginning. He proved that He didn't break His own rules of moral responsibility by not letting us "get away with it"; and He didn't just ignore the rules of right and wrong in the world He created. He didn't do wrong Himself—or let us do wrong without consequences.

He played the game so well that He accomplished the seemingly impossible (redemption and reconciliation) without capriciousness or divine injustice—to His Creation, or us. You may have thought God had disqualified Himself from His divine and moral position atop the cosmic "leader board" by not punishing every sin the minute it occurred—or at least during the lifetime of the sinner—but the Crucifixion of Jesus proves otherwise.

Sin was not ignored; it was punished properly, but in an unexpected way. And the result is that everybody wins—everybody, that is, who takes the gift of grace and mercy and applies it to his or her own score—which is allowed by the rules.

That's why we're here, of course: to celebrate the victory God won for us in Jesus Christ, and to relive the glory of that victory by gathering at His table and sharing the victory meal.

And so, let's do.

৵৽

3.

You *Can* Get There from Here

Romans 3:19-26 ESV

¹⁹ Now we know that whatever the law says it speaks to those who are under the law, so that every mouth may be stopped, and the whole world may be held accountable to God. ²⁰ For by works of the law no human being will be justified in his sight, since through the law comes knowledge of sin.

²¹ But now the righteousness of God has been manifested apart from the law, although the Law and the Prophets bear witness to it— ²² the righteousness of God through faith in Jesus Christ for all who believe. For there is no distinction: ²³ for all have sinned and fall short of the glory of God, ²⁴ and are justified by his grace as a gift, through the redemption that is in Christ Jesus, ²⁵ whom God put forward as a propitiation by his blood, to be received by faith. This was to show God's righteousness, because in his divine forbearance he had passed over former sins. ²⁶ It was to show his righteousness at the present time, so that he might be just and the justifier of the one who has faith in Jesus.

∽•∽

You've probably heard the old joke about the stranger who's driving along, out in the country, and realizes he has lost his way. He comes to an unmarked fork in the road with a fellow sitting on a fence nearby, watching him. The stranger calls out to the fellow on the fence and asks him how to get where he wants to go.

The fellow considers for a minute and then replies, "You could go down *that* road," pointing to his left. The driver waves his thanks and starts to put the car in gear, but before he can, the fellow continues, "Of course, *that's* a better road," pointing to his right.

A little exasperated, the driver acknowledges the extra information with another wave and prepares to drive off down the other road when the fellow says, "But the truth is, neither one of these roads will get you where you want to go. You can't get there from here."

❦❧

That's what it's like reading the first three chapters of Romans. There's the Apostle Paul, like the fellow on the fence, giving directions to everybody who shows up looking for the right way to go. Everybody, it turns out, is lost—though not all of them know it.

And Paul is giving directions, whether they ask for them or not, because Paul knows that just about everybody wants to know how to get where he or she needs to go—and absolutely everybody *needs* to know, but doesn't.

In Chapter 1, Paul points down one road and says, "You can go down that road—and a lot of people have. That road goes down through a dark and twisted valley. It's wide and smooth to start with, and the scenery is captivating. Go that way and it will be hard to keep your eyes on the road and your mind on where you want to end up. You keep going down that road and, after a while, you'll get more and more lost and the road will get more and more dangerous. Whatever you think of it now, it's really an awful road. We call it 'the way of the world.'"

In Chapter 2 of Romans, Paul points to the other road and says, "You could go up that road—a few people have. It's kind of a private road. The only people who ever take it are my relatives. It's a narrow road and pretty challenging from the beginning, even though it's a very straight road. It's a road that heads up a mountain, and you can get high enough to be able to see where you want to go.

"But the truth is that it's so steep in places that a lot of people who take it don't have the power to make the climb. A lot of people slide off the road. And those who manage to stay on the road get to the end of it only to realize that it doesn't go all the way over the mountain. It's a frustrating road. I know, I tried it for a long time. It's called, 'the way of the Law.'"

And there you sit, waiting for the punch line—waiting for Paul to say, "You can't get there from here."

Except, this time, it's no joke. There's nothing funny about the punch line when you're the stranger—when you're the one who's lost and doesn't know how to get where you need to go. It's not funny when it's the story of your life. It's not funny when you tried one of the roads—or both— and you know from experience they don't take you where you want and need to go. It's not funny—and Paul isn't laughing.

಄ೲ

It wouldn't matter so much if the "there" you're trying to get to wasn't so important.

But it is.

"There" is "home"—your Father's "house"⁹—the place where you belong and the only place where you will ever be truly happy. "There" is the place where you are loved unconditionally¹⁰ and where you will be eternally safe.¹¹ You and everybody else have tried to get there—some, in the worst possible way—and a few, in the best possible way you could think of or try.

---

⁹ John 14:2-3; Hebrews 4:9-11.
¹⁰ 1 John 4:13-17.
¹¹ Psalm 4:8.

And yet every road you or anybody else has tried ended up a dead end. You take the low road of this world and crash into all kinds of evil obstacles. You take the high road of moral legalism and stall on the steep slope of good intentions. Neither road takes you home.

Maybe you've come to that conclusion all by yourself. Maybe you don't need Paul to tell you, "You can't get 'there' from here." You can't get home to God living the life you've lived. You can't get "there," no matter which way you decide to go.

ঔ৵

Except Paul doesn't say that.

He says, "You couldn't get there from here—until now. You couldn't get there—but now, you can!" And Paul points the lost stranger—you—to a new road—a new way newly constructed— that wasn't there before. It is the way home. Now—you *can* get "there" from here.

No joke! It's God's honest—and saving—truth.

God has built a new road from His home to you, and this road will get you there, no matter what other road you've been on and how far down (or up) that road you've gone. Now, you *can* get "there" from here.

But how?

There is a praise chorus that proclaims:

> "God will make a way
>
> where there seems to be no way.
>
> He works in ways we cannot see.
>
> He will make a way for me."[12]

Jesus told His disciples the day before He died that *He* was the way. *"No one comes to the Father,"* He told them, *"except by me."*[13] God

---

[12] Don Moen, "God Will Make a Way," 2003.

[13] John 14:6, ESV.

made a way for you and me and everyone[14] to get "there" from here. Jesus is the way.

You can't get "there" going the way of the world, ignoring and rebelling against God. You can't get "there" going the way of works, trying to earn God's approval by doing good deeds.

All have sinned. All have fallen short of the glory of God. No one will get to the right place with God by anything he or she does.

There's only one way to get "there": the way of Jesus—the way of grace.[15] And everybody can get "there" that way. And that's what Paul is pointing to: the new way of God's grace in Jesus Christ.

❧

This road, according to Paul, is the way for all who believe. All who go this way will be justified—will get to the right place—will get "there" with God—even though we are all sinners and have fallen short in the divine glory department.

The reason this road is the right road—the reason it works when the other roads didn't—is that you don't "take" this road— it takes you. You are taken—on this road—by God. On this road, you don't do the driving like you did on the other roads to nowhere good.

On the road of God's grace, God does the driving. You can get "there," but you can't drive "there" yourself. To take this road, you let God take control and take you where He wants to take you.

❧

And where does the way of grace go?

According to Paul, it goes through the redemption that is in Christ Jesus. It is a road ploughed by the Cross and paved in the Savior's blood. It is a toll road of sorts: the toll—your toll—having

---

14 Matthew 18:14; 2 Peter 3:9.
15 Acts 4:12; Ephesians 2:8-9.

been paid in full by the sacrificial death of Jesus. The full cost of construction was covered by the priceless gift of God's Son.

And so it is a road that takes you home through faith in Jesus Christ—your faith that God has built this road and that He will let you come home by it—that He will carry you with Him to be where He is—where He always wanted you to be—at home—and right—with Him.

The way of grace—the way home with God—is for all who believe—for all who believe it is so—for all who accept the "ride" offered by God the Father on the road He has made possible for all of us through His Son Jesus Christ.

There is now a way for sinners—all of us—to be forgiven. There is now a way for all who have fallen short of God's glory to have all of that glory restored. There is a way now for the guilty to be "justified"—as Paul puts it—to get to the place where we are all right with God—where we are where God wants us to be and who God wants us to be.

There is a road, down which God will take us if we will let Him, where our faith in Jesus Christ will reflect God's faith in us. It's no joke—though it could make you laugh out loud, it's so wonderful!

�✺�

It's so wonderful, if you get the right directions and follow them. But not everybody comes to the fork in the road where Paul is waiting to give directions. And that's no laughing matter. *You* got the word. But how about "them"?

Imagine looking down the road of rebellion and not knowing it leads to destruction. Imagine the allure of all those festive folks honking their horns and waving out their windows as they race down that road to their doom with no one to warn them away from it.

Or can you picture the disappointment those brave, sad souls will experience who set out with the best of intentions to scale the unreachable peaks of perfect conduct, carefully observing the speed limits and all the other rules of the road all the way?

"You can't get 'there' that way," Paul would say to them.

But if Paul is not there to say it, who will?

Giving directions isn't that hard, if you know you *can* get "there" from here, and you know the only way that you—or anyone else —can get "there."

You know you can get there. And you know the way.

The way of the Cross—the way of Christ—leads home.[16]

಄ஃ

---

[16] Jessie Brown Pounds, "The Way of the Cross Leads Home," 1906.

Romans 5:1-8 NRSV

¹ *Therefore, since we have been justified by faith, we have peace with God through our Lord Jesus Christ.* ² *Through him we have also obtained access by faith into this grace in which we stand, and we rejoice in hope of the glory of God.* ³ *Not only that, but we rejoice in our sufferings, knowing that suffering produces endurance,* ⁴ *and endurance produces character, and character produces hope,* ⁵ *and hope does not put us to shame, because God's love has been poured into our hearts through the Holy Spirit who has been given to us.*

⁶ *For while we were still weak, at the right time Christ died for the ungodly.* ⁷ *For one will scarcely die for a righteous person—though perhaps for a good person one would dare even to die—* ⁸ *but God shows his love for us in that while we were still sinners, Christ died for us.*

৯৹৶

4.

Making Peace with Your Father

Romans 5:1-8 NRSV

Ladies, today's sermon is a Fathers' Day sermon, which might suggest to you that you get the week off, so to speak. But let me encourage you to pay close attention anyway, so that you will know when to lean over and whisper, "I told you so."

As a matter of fact, the fathers here today will be the "targets" for only part of the sermon. Everybody will get a turn in the crosshairs today because everyone has, or has had, a father, at least biologically, and therefore, also, psychologically. Most of us have known and lived with our fathers, physically as we grew up, and (again) psychologically for all our lives.

I emphasize the psychological dimension of our relationships with our fathers in both cases because, regardless of your age, and whether your father is living or dead, you are among the majority of people if your relationship with your father is still affecting your life, your perspectives, and your relationships with other people, for good or ill.

For far too many people—even Christian people—that relationship was, and continues to be, experienced as conflict. Though mothers can have difficult relationships with their children—and can fail to fulfill their maternal responsibilities—it is fathers who come to mind most often when we think of conflict in the family—of struggles between parent and child.

Now here let me say that for you who come to this day with fond and appreciative memories of a wonderful father, living or dead, we celebrate with you a rich and increasingly rare blessing. May God hallow the memory of such fathers who have departed this life, and sustain the health and happiness of those who are still with you.

And for the fathers here who have experienced success and satisfaction in your parenting efforts—who have seen your children grow in godly character and capability while enjoying a healthy and affirming relationship with them, we congratulate you on your special good fortune. Today we honor you and recognize that you have achieved what many men find very elusive.

But as Forrest Gump[17] would say, "That's all I've got to say about that."

❧

On the other hand, there is more to say, to fathers, and the sons and daughters of fathers, who view that relationship with frustration, anger, grief, disappointment, shame or other negative feelings. As much as you might like to castigate your father—if you think he deserves it—it is more important that you make peace with him.

That peace with earthly fathers is so difficult to attain should not surprise us. Conflict arose in the first family—and I don't mean the one that lives in the White House. The willful disobedience of Adam and Eve created conflict between them and their Heavenly Father (the only father they had, by the way).[18] And every descendant of Adam and Eve has been in conflict with God in the same way for the same reason.[19]

---

[17] Played by Tom Hanks, *Forrest Gump*, 1994.
[18] Genesis 3.
[19] Isaiah 53:6, Romans 3:10-12.

The story of the Bible, from the Garden of Eden to the Garden of Gethsemane,[20] has been the story of a Heavenly Father in conflict with His sinful children, fighting a war He did not chose and does not desire with sons and daughters who are determined to be rebellious. King David was a terrible father, but even he was grieved by the rebellion of his son, Absalom[21]—rebellion that ultimately destroyed his son, despite David's efforts to make peace and save him.[22]

You must make peace with your father, living or dead, because the conflict damages you, as long as it remains unresolved, no matter who is to blame. But to make peace with a human father, you first need to make peace with your Heavenly Father, because all of our conflicts with each other are really part of, and fueled by, our prior conflict with God.[23]

The good news is that you don't have to make peace with God so much as merely to accept the peace He has already made with you. As you heard earlier, Paul said that while we were the enemies of God—children in rebellion against our Father—God made peace with us. Our sin—our rebellion—required God to make war against us to preserve the system of morality and justice and order He created (for our benefit, by the way, as well as for His glory).

But in the crucifixion of Jesus Christ, the Heavenly Father gave up to death His most beloved Son to forge a truce—an armistice—peace. Though we do not deserve it—and could not compel it—we have been offered peace with God instead of war. Putting your faith in Jesus Christ and His sacrifice is the means of accepting the offer of peace with God. It is the means of eternal salvation, and the means of making peace with your Heavenly Father.

And in the safety of peace with God, you can make peace with the others you have been at war with, including, if need be, your

---

[20] Matthew 26:36-46.
[21] 2 Samuel 15:30.
[22] 2 Samuel 18:5, 9-15.
[23] Psalm 51:4; Matthew 5:23-24.

other father—the human one. Of course, when you are at peace with God, you are no longer alone in your efforts to make peace with others. His resources are made available to you for the interpersonal repairs that are needed, despite the fact that you used to be God's enemy.

It's something like "a divine Marshall Plan."

ॐॐ

After World War II, Europe lay in ruins from the fighting. The people were helpless. And yet, even the defeated countries received a massive amount of help from the victors to rebuild what had been destroyed. The help was given because the victors did not want to punish those who lost the war—even though they started it. The purpose of the great rebuilding was to overcome the hostility that had existed and to build relationships that would preserve the peace and bless everyone. Peace brought not just the end of conflict, but the gift of a new and better life.

Suppose you grew up with a father you found it hard to get along with. Let's say he did his best, but maybe he didn't understand you or appreciate your perspective, your dreams, or your friends. Maybe he wasn't much on conversation or too strict about "whatever."

Maybe he was too busy with other things too often. And maybe, because he wasn't perfect, he wasn't acceptable. Maybe he didn't measure up to someone else's dad, or the model in your mind of what you wanted him to be. And you cut yourself off from him, emotionally. You put as much distance between you and him as you could.

Now, however many years later, do you still hold on to the dissatisfaction? Or the disappointment? Does your frustration and impatience still flair up when you deal with him—or with situations—and people—that remind you of him and your relationship with him? And what good does it do—to you or anybody?

Perhaps he is long gone to his grave, but you are still struggling with the relationship—still in conflict.

It's time to make peace with your father.

ॐ॰ॐ

Now you are no longer a child; you have the understanding of experience. Let the wisdom God, your Heavenly Father, has given you guide you to see and appreciate the whole man your father was, not just the aspects you struggled with. Now you know the complexities of life as an adult and the difficulties of meeting your own financial and social and moral obligations when the right is not always clear, and the desirable is not always achievable, and your ability to satisfy the expectations of others—or even your own—is inadequate.

And what about your own contribution to the conflict? I do not intend to take you on a guilt trip, but rather, a journey of understanding. To make peace where there has been conflict—perhaps open warfare—you must see your own contribution to the process.

We all do the best we can with what we've got. We respond to our emotions and pursue the goals that seem important to us. But we can be shortsighted, and misguided, and driven by feelings that overwhelm reason and good judgment. This is especially true when we are children—and incredibly true when we are teenagers—or "adult trainees."

Making peace when your relationship was difficult requires a deeper, more gracious appreciation of both parties to the conflict, you and your father. The truth is: You can redefine its meaning, even now. You may recalculate the "grade" you gave your father. Even though you may never be able to have the kind of relationship you wanted, you may be able to accept the relationship in a new way that brings you a new peace with your father, or his memory, and with yourself. And because you have peace with God, your Heavenly Father, He will make up the difference between what you should do and want to do and what you are not able to do by yourself. He will give you peace with your earthly father, if you will let Him.

∔

Ah, but suppose your relationship with your father was not merely disappointing or difficult. In a group this size, it is not impossible that one or more of you grew up with a father who was abusive to you or other members of your family, or who was consumed by addictions or given to unfaithfulness.

There are fathers who destroy families, whose demonic behavior cannot and should not be understood or appreciated in its context. There are fathers who are no fathers—and worse. How can you make peace with that?

The Psalmist says, *"Though my father and mother forsake me, the Lord will receive me"*[24] and *"A father to the fatherless…is God.…"*[25] Paul reminds the Corinthians of God's age-old promise: *"'I will be a father to you, and you will be my sons and daughters,' says the Lord."*[26]

When you are at peace with God the Father—*your* Father— you are never without a father, whatever your human father may have done or been or failed to be. Your Father Who is in heaven[27] has forgiven all your sins and can give you the ability to forgive all the sins a dysfunctional earthly father committed against you,[28] even those that are far greater than any you have committed yourself. And however demonic your father may have been toward you, the substitute relationship with your Heavenly Father is, and will be, eternally—infinitely—more divine.

---

[24] Psalm 27:10, NIV.
[25] Psalm 68:5, NIV.
[26] 2 Corinthians 6:18, NIV (quoting 2 Samuel 7:14).
[27] Matthew 6:9.
[28] Matthew 6:12, 14.

When John focuses on this miracle of divine adoption, all he can do is exclaim, *"How great is the love the Father has lavished on us, that we should be called the children of God! And so we are!"* [29]

"We have peace with God through our Lord Jesus Christ." And in that peace—through Jesus Christ—we can make peace with other enemies—and end other wars that have scarred us for far too long. As a great general said after the worst war our country had ever endured: "Let us have peace." [30]

By the grace of God, let us have peace.

ॐ

---

[29] 1 John 3:1, NIV.
[30] Ulysses S. Grant, in accepting the Republican Party's nomination to be its candidate for President in 1868.

Romans 5:1-5 NRSV

[1] *Therefore, since we have been justified by faith, we have peace with God through our Lord Jesus Christ.* [2] *Through him we have also obtained access by faith into this grace in which we stand, and we rejoice in hope of the glory of God.* [3] *Not only that, but we rejoice in our sufferings, knowing that suffering produces endurance,* [4] *and endurance produces character, and character produces hope,* [5] *and hope does not put us to shame, because God's love has been poured into our hearts through the Holy Spirit who has been given to us.*

❧

5.

Peace, Grace, Glory and Love

Romans 5:1-5 NRSV

Today, we worship our God in the shadow of our country's remembrance of those who died in its defense.[31] We have shown the pictures of those in our Chapel family who have served—and are even now serving—in our military—to honor that service.

But tomorrow is dedicated to those who did even more—who gave up their very lives in war to protect our citizens and preserve our freedoms and way of life. Simply put: They died that we might live.

It has been said that only those who have experienced war can truly appreciate peace. And everyone who gave his life, gave it, ultimately, *for* peace—to overcome some great conflict with our enemies and end a war in our favor.

In recent years, the distinction between war and peace has become hazy and confused. We parse our words and blur the lines. Clarity is a casualty, and with it, common purpose. In earlier times, we knew the difference between the two.

When Franklin Roosevelt went before Congress the day after the Pearl Harbor attack, he asked those men and women for a

---

[31] This sermon was preached the Sunday of a Memorial Day weekend.

declaration of war: that, "since the unprovoked and dastardly attack...a state of war has existed."[32] And so they declared.

Almost four years later, when Douglas Macarthur stood on the deck of the battleship MISSOURI and concluded the ceremony that concluded the war, he issued what amounted to a declaration of peace, announcing, "These proceedings are closed." But before he said that, he offered this prayer: "Let us pray that peace be now restored to the world and that God will preserve it always."[33]

That war was over. Many had died so that there would be peace. Those who were spared gave thanks for the grace they had received. Those who had suffered looked through their suffering in hope to the glory of a better day.

కోపొడ

That was many years ago now, but the dramatic words of President Roosevelt and General MacArthur still grip the heart and stir the mind.

But even those words pale in comparison to what the Apostle Paul has to say in the fifth chapter of Romans.

The world was at war in Paul's day as well—at war with God. Paul acknowledged that a state of war existed between God on the one side and all of humanity on the other. God was at war with everyone who had launched unprovoked and dastardly attacks of sin on His holiness and righteousness and sovereign will.

That war continues around our world, but God is no longer at war with everyone. Peace has been restored between God and some in this world, and for those who are at peace with God, God will preserve that peace, always and forever.

In the war between the nations of the world, millions gave their lives in the cause of peace. In the war between God and the world, one Man gave His life to restore humanity's peace with God. Paul

---

[32] President Franklin D. Roosevelt, Washington, DC, December 8, 1941.
[33] General Douglas MacArthur, Tokyo Bay, Japan, September 2, 1945.

says that *"we have peace with God through our Lord Jesus Christ."* As Jesus hung on the Cross and gave His life for all those warring against God, He cried out, *"It is finished!* [34] The war is over! These proceedings are closed."

When the great book was closed aboard the USS MISSOURI, the war was over for all those who accepted the terms of the peace—for all those who *believed* the war was over.

And what did those who started the war, but could not win the war, receive from the victor?

Grace. Marvelous, unmerited grace.[35] Their sins were forgiven. Their wounds…tended. Their hungers…fed.

They surrendered and those who had been their unconquerable enemy restored their lives and rebuilt their homes and transformed their world in an unimaginably wonderful way.

But first, they had to surrender. First, they had to submit in faith to those they had hurt but could never defeat. They had to give up the fight.

Paul was writing to a community of those who had given up the fight against God—the fight they themselves had started. And God responded to their surrender not with retribution, but with reconciliation—not with punishment, but with peace. They have peace with God through the sacrifice of One Who gave His life in the service of that cause.

But peace with God was only the beginning. *"Through [our Lord Jesus Christ],"* wrote Paul, *"we have obtained access…to this grace in which we stand."*

[34] John 19:30, RSV.
[35] See Julia H. Johnston, "Marvelous Grace of Our Loving Lord," 1911.

In the fall of 1945, the Second World War was over. There was peace. As General MacArthur said aboard the MISSOURI, "A great tragedy has ended. A great victory has been won.... The holy mission has been completed."[36]

But the devastation of the war remained. Those who had started the war were destitute and had no means to repair the damage their sinful behavior had brought down upon them.

And the remarkable response of the victors came in the form of a great plan of reconstruction bearing the name of another general, George Marshall. "Our policy," he said, "is directed... against hunger, poverty, desperation, and chaos...."[37]

The Marshall Plan provided millions of people access to the resources they needed to survive, as ships and planes brought food and clothing, money and materials to build a new life. It gave them a future. It gave a broken world hope.

It was a shining example of human compassion and generosity bestowed on those who had so recently been the implacable foe. It was a remarkable act of grace.

ॐ

But here, too, the human pales beside the divine, because God Himself, through our Lord Jesus Christ, has satisfied the hunger, not merely of the body, but of the soul as well. He has put all the riches of heaven on the balance against our moral poverty.

Through our Lord Jesus Christ, we who were God's enemies are now supplied with all the resources of His grace, so that our spiritual desperation is dissolved in His "blessed assurance"—the chaos of sin's consequences is converted into great order and opportunity for a beloved child of God.

---

[36] MacArthur, op. sit., p. 28.

[37] George C. Marshall, American Secretary of State, "Against Hunger, Poverty, Desperation and Chaos," speech given at Harvard University, June 5, 1947.

God's "Messiah Plan" did not last for just a year or two; it endures forever. It is not limited to continent, country or clan; it extends to every nation, home and human heart.

Through our Lord Jesus Christ, we now have access to a "grace that is greater than all our sins"—greater than all the crushing consequences of all our sins.

And through our Lord Jesus Christ—Who ended our war with God on the Cross and opened the way to grace through His Resurrection—we are on our way to sharing the glory of God.

Though we were God's enemies, God has made us His beloved sons and daughters. And with the end of the war and the establishment of peace, it is only natural that we should come home.

ॐ⋅ॐ

General MacArthur told the American people at the end of the war, "And so, my fellow countrymen, today I report to you that your sons and daughters…are homeward bound—take care of them."[38]

And so they would: grand homecomings, parades of celebration, parties, programs and feasts.

And even before they arrived at home, whether they were to pass beside the statue in New York or beneath the bridge in San Francisco, those coming back from the war felt the growing sense of exhilaration and joy as the time and miles passed, and their destination (and the ones they loved most) drew nearer.

And for the Christian, who was the enemy of God and is now a beloved child, at peace with the Father—for the Christian who was defeated and destitute and is now properly and permanently positioned to receive God's grace—the journey home will one day position you there at the glorious throne of the Heavenly Father, to share in the celebration of your deliverance from your rebellion

---

[38] MacArthur, op. sit., p. 28.

into His eternal love. No matter where you go on the way—no matter what suffering you may encounter on the journey from sin through salvation to peace and grace, you endure it with hope for the glory of God that is to come, and the love of God that will never go away.

Is your war with God over?

His holy mission is complete. Surrender to His salvation and come home in peace to His glory, grace and love—through Jesus Christ our Lord, Amen.

৵৹

Romans 5:6-8 ESV

The Book of Romans is Paul's explanation of man's need—and God's gift—of salvation. In today's reading, Paul sums up what the Crucifixion means for us.

৯৶৻

⁶ For while we were still weak, at the right time Christ died for the ungodly. ⁷ For one will scarcely die for a righteous person—though perhaps for a good person one would dare even to die— ⁸ but God shows his love for us in that while we were still sinners, Christ died for us.

৯৶৻

John 15:12-17 ESV

On their last night together, Jesus promoted His followers from servants to friends and commanded them to love one another, defining "love" as the kind of sacrifice He would soon make for them. He also clarified the purpose for which He had chosen them: to go and bear lasting fruit.

ॐ~⚫

[Jesus said:]

¹² "This is my commandment, that you love one another as I have loved you. ¹³ Greater love has no one than this, that someone lay down his life for his friends. ¹⁴ You are my friends if you do what I command you. ¹⁵ No longer do I call you servants, for the servant does not know what his master is doing; but I have called you friends, for all that I have heard from my Father I have made known to you. ¹⁶ You did not choose me, but I chose you and appointed you that you should go and bear fruit and that your fruit should abide, so that whatever you ask the Father in my name, he may give it to you. ¹⁷ These things I command you, so that you will love one another."

ॐ~⚫

6.

To Love Like Jesus

Romans 5:6-8; John 15:12-17 ESV

It was 50 years ago this year that my father's mother got sick and died with cancer. In the last months of her life, we took her into our home and my mother cared for her. Hospice in those days was a family affair.

Momma Hill was beloved—*revered*, really—by her six surviving children, of whom my father was the eldest. The youngest, my Aunt Virginia, told me years later that in Momma Hill's final days, in her pain and delirium, she would clutch Virginia's hand and plead, "Will you die for me?"

And crushed by her mother's suffering, all Virginia could say was, "Momma, if I could, I would!"

෨ঞ

Across this country and around the world lie multitudes of men and women who died for you and me—in the abstract, at least. Many, no doubt, in the heat of battle, died for someone in particular, the soldier or Marine in the mud beside them—a shipmate at sea or crewmember in the air—the comrade in arms who had, in the crucible of war, become closer than a brother. That is a special kind of love.

It is the greatest kind of love, according to Jesus. To die for someone else—and more specifically, to lay down your life for someone—freely, voluntarily, sacrificially—is perhaps the noblest and most virtuous act a person can perform, which is why we view the graves at Arlington and Gettysburg and "Flanders Fields" and a hundred other places as hallowed ground.

When asked, "Will you die for me?" they answered, "Yes!"

This weekend we honor the memories of those who died for their country—for the cause of freedom—and for their friends.

And today, we use this duty-to-pay-tribute as a springboard to see an even greater example of the greatest kind of love—the love of Jesus for His disciples, His servants, His friends.

My Aunt Virginia wanted to take her mother's place and die because my grandmother had spent her life in sacrificial devotion to her children. The warriors who "took a bullet" for their buddies knew their buddies would have—and in many cases had—taken bullets for them.

ও⁈

But, as the Apostle Paul pointed out, *"Christ died for the ungodly.... While we were still sinners, Christ died for us."* Jesus laid down His life for 12 men—and the whole world—not because they or we had earned the favor and deserved the consideration, but because we had *not*, and could not. We had not poured a lifetime of selfless mother-love into Jesus or shared the hardships and hazards of warfare with Him. We were the enemy across the no-man's-land fighting off His every advance. We were the wayward and rebellious children breaking our Heavenly Father's heart at every turn.

Those who died in the service of our country believed they were fighting—and dying—for something worth the sacrifice. God sent Jesus to be the Christ Who would lay down His life for a human race God knew to be completely *un*worthy of His sacrificial love. God sent Jesus to lay down His life *because* we are unworthy. "We are not worthy so much as to gather up the crumbs under [His] Table"—as the prayer goes[39]—but still Jesus came. And still He called us His friends. And still He laid down His life for His friends—for us.

Jesus laid down His life for us—and so we live. We have dodged "the divine bullet" (or the demonic one, depending on your perspective). But either way, *"When you were dead in your sins...,"* wrote Paul, *"God made you alive with Christ."*[40]

"Thank you, Jesus! And so long, till next time!"

ஒ~ன்

But it's not as simple as that. Jesus laid down His life for us— He died for us. Now, having died for us—the unfriendly folks He called "friends"—He commands us to be friends like Him—to love like Him—to lay down our lives like Him.

The command is simple—and repeated for clarity and emphasis. *"God so loved the world...."*[41] And so should we. But we start by loving each other. Each of the 12 apostles was commanded to love the 11 other men (even Judas, apparently). Each of us is commanded to love the several hundred other people in this church.

"Love them? I don't even *know* some of them!"

Jesus said, *"Love each other as I have loved you."* Maybe you should spend a little time with the pictorial directory this afternoon and think about how you can love those people in the pictures the way Jesus loves you. Have you considered that your Savior has commanded you to love the people in the book and in the seats around you like He loves you? And have you considered what that means?

---

[39] From "The Prayer of Humble Access," in the Communion liturgy of *The Episcopal Book of Common Prayer*, 1928.
[40] Colossians 2:13, NIV.
[41] John 3:16, RSV.

You know what *you* think that means. Do you know what *Jesus* thinks it means? Do you think you're thinking the same thing as Jesus? What does He want His love to accomplish in your life? What does He want His love in you to accomplish in the lives of others—those He has commanded you to love as He has loved you?

Jesus isn't talking about loving the people you love. He's talking about loving each other—the other people who just happen to be the membership of this little mob of Christians we call "Trinity."

"*Love* 'um? I don't even *like* some of them!"

And maybe Jesus didn't like some of the disciples.

The Bible doesn't tell us that He liked them. It tells us, in fact, that He got mad at them—He got frustrated and exasperated with them. He rebuked them, corrected them, challenged them, instructed them—repeatedly, and at great lengths. He intervened in their squabbles. He predicted their denial and desertions, accepted one's betrayal...

...and died for them.

Jesus laid down His wonderful, sinless, miracle-working, divine-human life for them. Jesus chose to love them (and us) because that's what God sent Him to do—commanded Him to do—however He happened to feel about us—however our individual and collective personalities happened to strike Him.

Jesus didn't have to like me or my behavior or my attitude or my politics or anything else about me to love me and lay down His life for me. For that matter, He didn't have to love me and choose me as His friend to die for—except that His Heavenly Father commanded Him to—just as He has commanded me to love you and lay down my life for you.

Jesus didn't have to—except that He *did* have to if I was going to be "died for," as I had to be, if I wasn't going to have to die for myself, lost and condemned in my sin. Only Jesus could do what had to be done for me. And He did, by loving me enough (for God knows why) to lay down His life for me—and—for you.

అ•ଓ

What do you do when someone has laid down his life for you?

That's the question they finally come to at the end of the movie *Saving Private Ryan*,[42] which will certainly be on TV somewhere this weekend. One soldier is chosen (at the highest level) to be saved from the horrors of war, and others are ordered to seek him and save him[43]—a stranger—even if they must lay down their own lives to do so—which, in the end, they all do.

What do you do? What do you do when someone has died for you?

That's what Private Ryan asks as he kneels before the cross of the man who accomplished his rescue—the man who died to ensure that he would live.

The best answer the film makers could come up with was: Live a good life—be a good person.

Jesus has a better answer—perhaps because the life He laid down for His friends was a greater, purer, nobler sacrifice than even the ones depicted in the movie.

What do you do when this particular Someone has died for you?

You spend the rest of your life loving others as you have been loved by your Savior, laying down your life each day in a love like Jesus loved you with—going and bearing fruit—planting and cultivating in others that same lay-down-your-life love that Jesus—and His friends—have laid down in their lives for you.

అ•ଓ

---

[42] Movie *Saving Private Ryan*, 1998.
[43] Luke 19:10.

Romans 6:1-11 NRSV

[1] What shall we say then? Are we to continue in sin that grace may abound? [2] By no means! How can we who died to sin still live in it? [3] Do you not know that all of us who have been baptized into Christ Jesus were baptized into his death? [4] We were buried therefore with him by baptism into death, in order that, just as Christ was raised from the dead by the glory of the Father, we too might walk in newness of life.

[5] For if we have been united with him in a death like his, we shall certainly be united with him in a resurrection like his. [6] We know that our old self was crucified with him in order that the body of sin might be brought to nothing, so that we would no longer be enslaved to sin. [7] For one who has died has been set free from sin. [8] Now if we have died with Christ, we believe that we will also live with him. [9] We know that Christ, being raised from the dead, will never die again; death no longer has dominion over him. [10] For the death he died he died to sin, once for all, but the life he lives he lives to God. [11] So you also must consider yourselves dead to sin and alive to God in Christ Jesus.

છ-ન્ડ

7.

Dead to Sin—Alive to God

Romans 6:1-11 NRSV

In this passage from Romans, Paul is picking a fight with the people who figure that if God is so good at forgiving sin—and so willing to do so—they ought to give Him as much opportunity as possible to exercise that divine inclination, especially since our human inclination is to commit sin rather than resist it. It's an argument that drives Paul up a wall, and there are still people today who are making it.

It would be one thing if we were merely "passing strangers": You step on God's toes or bump into Him as you're going about your business and you say, "Excuse me," or "Sorry about that," and God says, "That's all right," or "No problem." And that's the end of it—except that you do it a lot and God always gives you a pass without getting aggravated and shoving you back, because God's a decent guy and all.

But the logic of this "sin all you want" argument breaks down when you factor in the fact that, as a Christian, you are forgiven because you are *"in Christ Jesus."*

Paul says, *"[you] were baptized into his death…buried with him…into death…united with him in a death like his."* Whatever you're doing now, you're doing it with Christ.

And when you decide to sin, despite His good advice and warnings and urging otherwise, you drag Him into whatever you get yourself into. Jesus said, *"as you have done…unto…the least of these…"* (which, I might add, includes yourself), *you have done…unto me."*[44] It's not a pretty picture, and ought to be enough to demolish the idea that we should embrace a sinful lifestyle so God can rack up "grace points."

Christ died for sin—our sin. He accepted the penalty price of death that sin imposes on everyone, even though He had not sinned.[45] That's why Paul says He died *"once for all."* But Paul also says, *"He died to sin."*

It gets a little complicated here, but what Paul means is that dying is the only way to get out of the control of sin. If you're dead, you don't feel the urge to satisfy the selfish and destructive desires that sin stimulates all the time.

The downside is that if you experience normal human death, you don't feel any other urges either, good or bad. You're dead and that's "it" as far as life on earth is concerned.

⇛

But Jesus didn't just die. God raised Him from the dead after He died.

Anybody can die. Everybody will, until Jesus returns. But if you attach yourself to Jesus the way Paul is talking about (through faith demonstrated in baptism), you attach your life to His like a train car is attached to a powerful locomotive engine, and you go wherever He takes you.

The first place Jesus takes you, of course, is to and through death. His physical death on the Cross becomes *your* death—the death of your life that is enslaved to sin where sin totally controls your desires, your attitudes and your actions.

---

[44] Matthew 25:40, KJV.
[45] 2 Corinthians 5:21.

Paul says, "Your sinful body is destroyed."

The term Paul uses for "destroyed" really means something like "rendered powerless." It's like taking the batteries out or pulling the plug on sin's power to run your life (because *that* life is dead). We are baptized into *that* death with Jesus, and so we have died to sin as well.

If we are dead to sin, it's like we don't hear the signal anymore, because the signal isn't getting through, because we unplugged the radio.

Or better yet, it's like "Caller ID." You hear the ringing, the temptation, but when you look and see who it is, you say, "Oh, it's sin again. Don't answer it."

In Christ, you are no longer a sucker for sin. Before you were baptized into Christ Jesus, sin would say, "Hey, try this!"

And you would say, "Uh, okay."

And wham! It would blow up in your face—or your heart—or your character—or your relationships.

You know the old saying: "Fool me once, shame on you. Fool me twice, shame on me." Well, sin just keeps on fooling us all our lives—because the old sinful nature in us wants to be fooled—until Jesus dies to sin and we die to sin with Him.

Paul says, *"you must consider yourself dead to sin."* This doesn't mean *"act* like you are." It means "realize that even though you *weren't*—now, as a Christian, you actually *are.*" There was line in a pop song some years ago that went,

> "I can see clearly now;
> the rain is gone."[46]

When you die to sin with Christ, the reign of sin over you is gone and you can see clearly what you could not see before: that your life means something else. You see yourself as God sees you and you see God as He intends for you to see Him.

❧

---

[46] Johnny Nash, "I Can See Clearly Now," 1972.

And Paul says one other thing: *"Consider yourself*—realize that you are—*dead to sin and **alive to God in Jesus Christ**."*

As a flower will turn to the sun, so believers turn their lives to God so that He is the focus of their attention and the fulfillment of all their genuine and healthy needs.

"We have been united with him in a death like his. We shall certainly be united with him in a resurrection like his." "If we have died with Christ, we… shall also live with him."

"Alive to God in Christ Jesus" means the circuit is open and His divine power is flowing—to you, and through you, to empower you. That's why Paul says in Philippians: *"I can do all things through him who strengthens me."*[47]

"Sin big" so God can forgive more?

"No way!" says Paul. *"Walk in newness of life."*

You are dead to sin and alive to God—just like Jesus.

෨෯

---

[47] Philippians 4:13, RSV.

Romans 6:3-11 ESV

³ Do you not know that all of us who have been baptized into Christ Jesus were baptized into his death? ⁴ We were buried therefore with him by baptism into death, in order that, just as Christ was raised from the dead by the glory of the Father, we too might walk in newness of life.

⁵ For if we have been united with him in a death like his, we shall certainly be united with him in a resurrection like his. ⁶ We know that our old self was crucified with him in order that the body of sin might be brought to nothing, so that we would no longer be enslaved to sin. ⁷ For one who has died has been set free from sin. ⁸ Now if we have died with Christ, we believe that we will also live with him. ⁹ We know that Christ, being raised from the dead, will never die again; death no longer has dominion over him. ¹⁰ For the death he died he died to sin, once for all, but the life he lives he lives to God. ¹¹ So you also must consider yourselves dead to sin and alive to God in Christ Jesus.

෧~෧

Matthew 28:1-10 ESV

[1] *Now after the Sabbath, toward the dawn of the first day of the week, Mary Magdalene and the other Mary went to see the tomb.* [2] *And behold, there was a great earthquake, for an angel of the Lord descended from heaven and came and rolled back the stone and sat on it.* [3] *His appearance was like lightning, and his clothing white as snow.* [4] *And for fear of him the guards trembled and became like dead men.* [5] *But the angel said to the women, "Do not be afraid, for I know that you seek Jesus who was crucified.* [6] *He is not here, for he has risen, as he said. Come, see the place where he lay.* [7] *Then go quickly and tell his disciples that he has risen from the dead, and behold, he is going before you to Galilee; there you will see him. See, I have told you."* [8] *So they departed quickly from the tomb with fear and great joy, and ran to tell his disciples.* [9] *And behold, Jesus met them and said, "Greetings!" And they came up and took hold of his feet and worshiped him.* [10] *Then Jesus said to them, "Do not be afraid; go and tell my brothers to go to Galilee, and there they will see me."*

৵৽

8.

His Resurrection—and Yours

Romans 6:3-11; Matthew 28:1-10 ESV

Easter: The Resurrection Day of Jesus. Crucified on the Cross. Buried in the tomb. Raised from the dead.

Easter: The Resurrection of Jesus—and everything that means. Preachers around the world today will proclaim it. Sunday School teachers will explain it. Apologists will defend it. Believers will rejoice over it as the greatest thing in the world—which it is.

The Resurrection of Jesus is the bedrock core of Christianity. It is the heart of the gospel of salvation—the main thing we tell the world about Jesus, and the main thing we take to heart about what *we* have been told. On this day, more than any other, we celebrate the Resurrection of Jesus, the miracle to which all the mighty acts of God in history before it moved and pointed.

Because of His Resurrection, we recognize that Jesus is Christ and Lord and God. Because of His Resurrection, we know that, in all Jesus said, God was speaking powerfully and truthfully to us— and in all Jesus did, He intentionally and accurately demonstrated God's divine nature, and God's eternal purpose for His Creation.

☙❧

Jesus was dead—as dead as you can get. And then, He was *alive*—and *is* alive—and will always *be* alive—forever. His Resurrection guarantees it.

And how wonderful for Jesus! He is alive again—as alive as we are, and yet, infinitely more alive than we are, because His life no longer awaits death as its inevitable conclusion. For Jesus, death no longer colors every consideration with the perspective imposed by the lurking fear of a final day—a final breath—a final flash of consciousness before all is lost in a darkness that never ends.

No, Jesus has been raised from the dead—from that death. And we celebrate for Him.

It couldn't have happened to a nicer guy—or one more deserving.

In fact, except for Jesus, it couldn't have happened to anyone deserving at all—because no one else was, or is.

༅

But the greatest thing about the Resurrection of Jesus is not what it means for Jesus. The greatest thing about the Resurrection of Jesus—the reason Easter Sunday is such a glorious day—is what His Resurrection means for *you*.

To put it simply: His Resurrection is the guarantee of *yours*—if you believe in His, and in the promise of the One Who raised Him *to raise you, too.*

So, on this Easter, this Resurrection Day (of Jesus), let us consider—and celebrate—*your* Easter, *your* resurrection day.

That's what Paul is doing in the portion of his letter to the believers in Rome that we read earlier: *"...we shall certainly be united with him in a resurrection like his."*

It's not unusual to think about your own death, especially if you've got a lot of life in your rearview mirror, or if your health or your work or your circumstances make it more possible, or even likely, that your death will not be a long way off. But how often and how deeply do you think about your own resurrection?

Let's think about it now.

The Bible is pretty clear that you've got a resurrection coming.

Jesus said, *"For this is the will of my Father, that everyone who looks on the Son and believes in him should have eternal life, and I will raise him up on the last day."*[48]

Paul wrote, *"Jesus died and rose again. Even so—through Jesus—God will bring with him those who have fallen asleep. For the Lord himself will descend from heaven with a cry of command, with the voice of an archangel, and with the sound of the trumpet of God. And the dead in Christ will rise...."*[49]

Paul told the Corinthians, *"God raised the Lord and will also raise us up by his power."*[50]

Here's how it works: If you believe in the Resurrection of Jesus, you've got a resurrection of your own coming.

And what is *your* resurrection going to be like?

Paul says, *"What is sown* (meaning your physical body, which he likens to a seed)*—What is sown is perishable; what is raised is imperishable. It is sown in dishonor; it is raised in glory. It is sown in weakness; it is raised in power. It is sown a natural body; it is raised a spiritual body. ...in a moment, in the twinkling of an eye, at the last trumpet. For the trumpet will sound, and the dead will be raised imperishable, and we shall be changed."*[51]

So, when you are raised from the dead, you will never have to "deal" with death again. You will be im-perish-able.

What's more: When you are raised from the dead, there will be nothing about you that will, in any way, embarrass you, frustrate you, disappoint you, or diminish you. Everything about you will be perfect. You will be completely covered in the glory of God.

When you are raised from the dead, not only will you not have to struggle with all the things you could not do well enough—or at all—in this life—not only will there be no temptations to contend

---

[48] John 6:40, ESV.
[49] 1 Thessalonians 4:14, 16, ESV.
[50] 1 Corinthians 6:14, ESV.
[51] 1 Corinthians 15:42-44, 52, ESV.

with. You will always and forever be able to do everything you need and want to do—and do them absolutely perfectly. And the only things you will want to do are the things you should do. You will know and remember and understand, just as perfectly, everything you should and want to know and remember and understand.

People accumulate weaknesses over the course of this life. You will be raised by and in God's infinite spiritual power with no weaknesses when you are resurrected.

Your resurrection will be spectacular, far more so than the relatively subdued Resurrection Jesus experienced. When you are raised from the dead, the whole world will know it immediately. Jesus will be there in all His divine majesty to raise you up. Angels will fill the sky. And trumpets will sound from heaven like no sound ever heard on earth.

And when He raises you to life again, you will know, immediately, that you are "you"—and you will know just as certainly that you are more than you ever were before—because when you are raised from the dead, you will be changed. You will be imperishable, glorious, powerful, spiritual.

On Easter Sunday, Christians sing, "Up from the grave He arose!"[52] On *your* resurrection day, you and all those who will be raised with you can sing, "Up from the grave *we* arose!"

> "Low in the grave *we* lay—
> (like) Jesus my Savior!
> Waiting the coming day—
> (of) Jesus my Lord!"

And then, on that day:

> "Up from the grave *we* arose,
> With a mighty triumph o'er *our* foes.
> *We* arose the victor[s] from the dark domain,
> And *we* live forever with His saints to reign.
> He arose! *We* arose!

---

[52] George C. Hugg, "He Arose," 1891.

Hallelujah!

Christ—*and we*—arose!

Am I being silly—or sacrilegious?

I don't think so.

The Son of God did not give up His exalted place in heaven and come to this earth and endure all that He endured—including and especially His Crucifixion[53]—so that *He* could be raised. He did all that—went through all that—for *your* resurrection. He died so that *you* could be raised. He was raised so that *you* would be, too. Otherwise, how would you know to believe—in His Resurrection—*and* yours?

Do you believe in the Resurrection of Jesus?

If so, you've got a resurrection of your own coming.

Guaranteed!

છ-જી

But what about now? What about this time between His Resurrection and yours? What about every day you have left in this life that is anything but what you've been promised for the next?

The truth is that His Resurrection has benefits for you even before you experience the resurrection He made possible for you. Before His Crucifixion, Jesus lived His life with an unwavering conviction that the God Who sent Him would preserve Him for eternity—come what may in this life.

And in like manner, with similar conviction, we sing:

"Because He lives, I can face tomorrow.

Because He lives, all fear is gone.

Because I know He holds the future—

Life is worth the living, just because He lives."[54]

Because Jesus lives, you know that your resurrection is right around the corner—and that *until* you turn that corner—that last

---

[53] Philippians 2:5-8.
[54] Bill Gaither, "Because He Lives," 1999.

corner of *this* life—tomorrow—and every tomorrow after that—will be a day spent in the loving fellowship—and the joyful service—of Jesus Christ, your Risen Savior.

Because He lives, everything you would normally and reasonably be afraid of is redefined as something that He has the power and will to overcome for you—something that you will one day leave behind—something you *can* leave behind because it will not be a part of the eternal life you spend with Him—something that is not a part of the future He holds in trust for you in anticipation of your resurrection.[55]

Because Jesus lives, even *this* life is worth living.

భం•ఈ

But, of course, you're not really living *this* life any more. You gave it up—crucified it—buried it—with Jesus—so that you could have a resurrected life like His, instead.

What did Paul say?

"We know that our old self was crucified with him.... We were buried... with him by baptism into death, in order that, just as Christ was raised from the dead by the glory of the Father, we, too, might walk in newness of life. Now, if we have died with Christ...we will also live with him."

Did Jesus have to wait *until* He was resurrected to live like He would when He *was* resurrected? Or did His faith in His Heavenly Father enable Him to live that eternal life with its remarkable power, glory and wonder in the midst of the frustration, frailty and fleetingness of this life?

And does *your* faith in the Resurrection of Jesus not enable you—and entitle you—to live your life like He lived His—to live your life in *this* world as "a foretaste of glory divine"?[56]

---

55 1 Peter 1:3-9.
56 Fanny Crosby, "Blessed Assurance," 1873.

Because His resurrection in the past guarantees your resurrection in the future, the assurance of your resurrection in the future transforms the life you are living in the present.

What do we say on Easter Sunday?

"Christ is Risen!" ("He is Risen, indeed!")

Well, because of that—if you believe *that*—*you* are risen!

You are risen, indeed!

൞

Romans 7:14-25 ESV

[14] *For we know that the law is spiritual, but I am of the flesh, sold under sin.* [15] *For I do not understand my own actions. For I do not do what I want, but I do the very thing I hate.* [16] *Now if I do what I do not want, I agree with the law, that it is good.* [17] *So now it is no longer I who do it, but sin that dwells within me.* [18] *For I know that nothing good dwells in me, that is, in my flesh. For I have the desire to do what is right, but not the ability to carry it out.* [19] *For I do not do the good I want, but the evil I do not want is what I keep on doing.* [20] *Now if I do what I do not want, it is no longer I who do it, but sin that dwells within me.*

[21] *So I find it to be a law that when I want to do right, evil lies close at hand.* [22] *For I delight in the law of God, in my inner being,* [23] *but I see in my members another law waging war against the law of my mind and making me captive to the law of sin that dwells in my members.* [24] *Wretched man that I am! Who will deliver me from this body of death?* [25] *Thanks be to God through Jesus Christ our Lord! So then, I myself serve the law of God with my mind, but with my flesh I serve the law of sin.*

ॐ•ॐ

Matthew 11:16-19, 25-30 ESV

[Jesus said:]

¹⁶ *"But to what shall I compare this generation? It is like children sitting in the marketplaces and calling to their playmates,*

> ¹⁷ *'We played the flute for you,*
> *and you did not dance;*
> *we sang a dirge,*
> *and you did not mourn.'*

¹⁸ *For John came neither eating nor drinking, and they say, 'He has a demon.'* ¹⁹ *The Son of Man came eating and drinking, and they say, 'Look at him! A glutton and a drunkard, a friend of tax collectors and sinners!' Yet wisdom is justified by her deeds."*

²⁵ *At that time Jesus declared, "I thank you, Father, Lord of heaven and earth, that you have hidden these things from the wise and understanding and revealed them to little children;* ²⁶ *yes, Father, for such was your gracious will.* ²⁷ *All things have been handed over to me by my Father, and no one knows the Son except the Father, and no one knows the Father except the Son and anyone to whom the Son chooses to reveal him.* ²⁸ *Come to me, all who labor and are heavy laden, and I will give you rest.* ²⁹ *Take my yoke upon you, and learn from me, for I am gentle and lowly in heart, and you will find rest for your souls.* ³⁰ *For my yoke is easy, and my burden is light."*

જી•સ્

9.

A Little Short of Perfection

Romans 7:14-25; Matthew 11:16-19, 25-30 ESV

When I was a child in grammar school, or elementary school, or whatever they call the early grades now, I was able, once or twice, to complete a year with perfect attendance. The achievement was so indicated on my report card.

Back then, report cards also had a place to grade "Conduct"—behavior in the classroom and on the playground. I—I regret to say—never attained perfection in my personal behavior in school. My conduct in class never merited the top mark.

I say this with regret, because it was never my intention to misbehave—I never meant to mess up.

But day after day, that's exactly what I did. I wanted to be good—to do what I was supposed to do—to get that perfect grade—but somehow, I couldn't. It was so frustrating—and not only for me.

One Friday afternoon, my fifth-grade teacher called me up to her desk as the other students were leaving and told me in no uncertain terms that she wanted to know "why I was the way I was," and that I had better think about that long and hard over the weekend because she expected me to have a good answer when I came back to class on Monday.

And I did think long and hard about it over the weekend, and I wondered what I would tell her. Then, late Sunday night, after having spent the better part of the day in church listening to sermons and Sunday School lessons, an answer came to me.

Monday morning, I strode cheerfully into class, and I told my teacher with all the theological *gravitas* I could muster in the face of her stern stare, "This is just how God made me."

My very impatient teacher wasn't very impressed with that answer. And as the years have gone by, I have become less impressed with it myself. God didn't make me imperfect. I did it myself.

❧

But I had help.

And as the years have gone by, I have discovered another frustration: I am not getting any closer to perfection in my personal behavior. I certainly discarded some of my pre-adolescent propensities as I got older, but I was only "trading up"—taking on more subtle and sophisticated imperfections to replace the ones I had outgrown.

I still want to be good—to do what I am supposed to do. And I understand what the good is far better now than I did when I was a ten-year-old boy. But time after time, even now, I don't do what I should do—what I want to do. "Conduct" is still—I regret to say—*not* my best subject.

I'm not even sure if I've done right by sharing all this with you. I don't normally bring my personal stories into sermons. The authority is in the Bible—not in me or my personal experiences. But today, I've spoken at length in the first personal singular because that's what the Apostle Paul has done.

Paul begins by reminding the Roman Christians of a shared understanding: *"We know that the law is spiritual...."* But from then on, it's all "I."

"I am of the flesh.... I do not understand my own actions.... I do not do what I want.... I do the very thing I hate.... I have the desire to do what is right, but [I do] not [have] the ability to carry it out."

"I – I – I – I – I."

Or, perhaps, *"I –* yie *– yie –* yie *– yie!"*

This may be Paul talking—and it sounds pretty personal. But I suspect that Paul has written this as a script for a part that just about anybody can play. And maybe that's Paul's point: "This is my story. But it is also yours. Step up to the microphone and read your lines—or better yet, recite them from memory—you know them by heart, anyway."

"I do not do what I want. I do the very thing I hate. I want to do right, but I don't. I try and I can't! I just don't understand."

You could say, "Well, this is just how God made me."

రా•ా

But that's not what the Bible says.

Here's what the Bible says about that: *"God created man in his own image, in the image of God he created him; male and female he created them.... And God saw everything that he had made, and behold, it was very good."*[57]

Why I am the way I am is not God's fault. He created me good—and able to do good.

But that's not the way it is now. The way I am is not the way God made me. God didn't make me imperfect. I did that myself.

It was kind of like this: *"...when the woman saw that the tree was good for food, and that it was a delight to the eyes, and that the tree was to be desired to make one wise, she took of its fruit and ate, and she also gave some to her husband who was with her, and he ate."*[58]

And then later, when they couldn't hide from God what they'd done...

---

[57] Genesis 1:27, 31, RSV.
[58] Genesis 3:5, RSV.

"*The man said, 'The woman whom you gave to be with me, she gave me fruit of the tree, and I ate.'*

"*Then the* LORD *God said to the woman, 'What is this that you have done?'*

"*The woman said, 'The serpent deceived me, and I ate.'*"[59]

I've eaten the forbidden fruit—some form of it—and so have you. God didn't make me imperfect; I did it myself. And I'm still doing it, every day.

But as with Adam and Eve, I've had help. In the Garden, it was the serpent, focusing their attention on God's law and then twisting it into a slick and cynical temptation. For you and me and everybody else, it is the sinister reality the serpent represents: sin.

Paul says, "*I am…sold under sin. …sin dwells within me. …evil lies close at hand. …making me captive to the law of sin that dwells in my members.*"

"*I am…sold under sin*"—like a slave bought to be abused by a sadistic master.

"*Sin dwells within me*"—like a parasite spreading a plague of improper impulses throughout my body.

"*Evil lies close at hand,*" waiting to lunge out and wreck whatever good intention I might have wanted to undertake.

"*The law of sin dwells in my members.*"

Sin has us all. It had Paul, who could say of his life before he met Christ: "*…as to righteousness under the law, blameless.…*"[60] Blameless—perfect score in conduct—and yet the Risen Christ could ask him, "*Why do you persecute me?*"[61]

❧

Now Paul knows better. Now he knows that his Law—the Law of Moses—a Law given by God Himself—can't make you good when sin is determined to make you bad. All the Law can do

---

[59] Genesis 3:12-13, ESV.
[60] Philippians 3:6, RSV.
[61] Acts 9:4-5, RSV.

is let you know what is bad and what is good. But sin even twists that so that you can think bad is good, and vice versa.

Jiminy Cricket was wrong: You can't "always let your conscience be your guide"[62]—not when it's been infected and corrupted by sin.

I want to do good, but I don't. I *don't* want to do wrong, and there I am, doing it again and again. I can't even be sure that I know the difference between good and evil when I'm staring it in the face and looking it up in the Bible!

Paul had thought he was "good to go" if he hitched his religious wagon to the Law of God.

What he didn't realize, but came to understand through his encounter with Jesus Christ, was that sin had a law, too. And sin has more power to enforce its law of evil than we have to live by the Law of God. Sin has the law-of-good-and-evil-by-itself beat.

It's enough to make you throw in the towel. As Paul put it: *"Oh, wretched man that I am! Who will deliver me*—from what sin is doing to me and my life?"

And just when it sounds like Paul has given up—just when it looks like there's nothing I can do about what sin is doing with me except take my failing grade in "conduct" and live with it—another Power enters the playground that sin has claimed.

"Who will deliver me" from this "bully" in my body who beats me down every day—this sin?

❧

And the answer is Jesus Christ—Jesus Christ, Paul's Lord—Jesus Christ, my Lord—Jesus Christ, your Lord—Jesus Christ, the Power of God that the Law of God—as wonderful as it was when not warped by sin—simply did not possess. Jesus has the power, and has exercised the power, to put sin in its place.

---

[62] Movie *Pinocchio*, 1950.

Now I know that there is another Power—a Power infinitely stronger than sin—at work on this "imperfection problem" of mine. Jesus has demonstrated His power over sin—and its henchman, death. Jesus has broken their stranglehold on me and my behavior and determined that their power will one day be no more.

Yes, sin is still a bother—still messing with me and undermining my desire and my efforts to perform to perfection for God.

But that's all right. My spirit is under God's control and I have learned that my desire to please Him is now sufficient, through Christ, to do just that. And because Jesus has placed my spirit under God's control, the sin still lurking in me physically doesn't have anything like the influence it used to have.

Sin no longer operates uncontested within me. It doesn't drive me to distraction and despair the way it used to when I was trying to be good without the power to pull it off. I no longer worry about the answer I'm going to give to the question of "why I am the way I am"—why I am anything but perfect.

Yes, it's my fault. I did it myself—with the enthusiastic encouragement of sin. And yes, Jesus said, *"You...must be perfect, as your heavenly Father is perfect."*[63]

But the Bible also says, *"...by a single offering [Jesus] has perfected for all time those who are being sanctified."*[64]

And so when Jesus Christ my Lord says, *"Come to me, all who labor and are heavy laden, and I will give you rest. Take my yoke upon you, and learn from me, for I am gentle and lowly in heart,"* I'm coming—with all the joy and confidence of a kid coming home with an unexpected "A+" on his report card in "Conduct."

છે•ઉ

---

[63] Matthew 5:48, RSV.
[64] Hebrews 10:14, ESV.

Romans 8:1-11 ESV

^{1} *There is therefore now no condemnation for those who are in Christ Jesus.* ^{2} *For the law of the Spirit of life has set you free in Christ Jesus from the law of sin and death.* ^{3} *For God has done what the law, weakened by the flesh, could not do. By sending his own Son in the likeness of sinful flesh and for sin, he condemned sin in the flesh,* ^{4} *in order that the righteous requirement of the law might be fulfilled in us, who walk not according to the flesh but according to the Spirit.* ^{5} *For those who live according to the flesh set their minds on the things of the flesh, but those who live according to the Spirit set their minds on the things of the Spirit.* ^{6} *For to set the mind on the flesh is death, but to set the mind on the Spirit is life and peace.* ^{7} *For the mind that is set on the flesh is hostile to God, for it does not submit to God's law; indeed, it cannot.* ^{8} *Those who are in the flesh cannot please God.*

^{9} *You, however, are not in the flesh but in the Spirit, if in fact the Spirit of God dwells in you. Anyone who does not have the Spirit of Christ does not belong to him.* ^{10} *But if Christ is in you, although the body is dead because of sin, the Spirit is life because of righteousness.* ^{11} *If the Spirit of him who raised Jesus from the dead dwells in you, he who raised Christ Jesus from the dead will also give life to your mortal bodies through his Spirit who dwells in you.*

૎્

10.

Full Pardon

Romans 8:1-11 ESV

From time to time, a trial will capture the imagination of the country. The media will get hold of it and fill the courtroom with microphones and cameras. Millions will watch as witnesses testify, and lawyers argue about the guilt or innocence of the accused. Fascinated viewers will make up their minds and pass their own judgment from the comfort of their easy chairs: "Guilty! Guilty as sin!"

And then one day, the trial is over and the only verdict that matters is announced. The verdict that will determine the fate of the defendant is read out for all to hear. Judgment hangs in the balance, and severe punishment will follow if the verdict is "Guilty." Everybody knows the person on trial is guilty. It's obvious. And so, how stunning when the verdict rendered is "Not Guilty."

"What kind of justice is that?!"

Now suppose the person on trial is not some famous athlete or slimy politician or monstrous young mother. Suppose the person on trial is *you*. Suppose you are the one who has been brought to justice—you are the one being held accountable for all the things you've done wrong—every evil deed—every wicked thought. There you are, helpless before the power of the court, and you are guilty—obviously guilty—guilty as sin—guilty *of* sin.

And the sentence for your crimes against the law of God?

Well, *"the wages of sin is death."*[65] And don't think there'll be any mitigation for good behavior. You are incapable of any behavior that would be good enough to mitigate any part of the punishment you're due. And the Judge is a big Believer in justice—He wrote the Law Himself. It doesn't look good for you.

"The defendant will stand for the reading of the verdict."

Does your pulse quicken? Does your chest get tight? Do your palms feel clammy and your throat dry?

ॐ

Not if you are *"in Christ Jesus."*

If you are *"in Christ Jesus,"* you know what the verdict is going to be. You know that the Judge is going to say *"Not* guilty." No matter what the charges or the evidence—no matter how damning the case against you—*"there is now no condemnation for those who are in Christ Jesus."* The only possible verdict is "Not guilty"—if you are *"in Christ Jesus."*

Let's clarify what that means.

There is now no condemnation by God of you for your sins. There *was* absolute and eternal condemnation. But there isn't now. And there never will be again—ever. There is not a little less condemnation—or even a lot less. There is *no* condemnation. None. Absolutely zero condemnation. You will not—cannot—be condemned—punished—for the sins you have committed, or will commit, in this life—no matter what—if you are *"in Christ Jesus."*

ॐ

On the other hand, if you are not *"in Christ Jesus,"* there is also only one possible verdict that the divine Judge can impose on you.

---

[65] Romans 3:23, RSV.

And it is not the one you want to hear. The Gospel of John makes it pretty clear: *"Whoever believes in him (*meaning Jesus, the only begotten Son of God*) is not condemned, but whoever does not believe stands condemned already...."*[66]

In God's courtroom, you are not "innocent until proven guilty"; you are guilty until *rendered* innocent. God knows every sin you ever committed and has determined that every one of those sins deserves condemnation. *You* deserve condemnation for every one of them. God knows what the Law requires; He wrote the Law. And He enforces it, righteously. God's judgment is never pretty for those who are not *"in Christ Jesus."*

"In Christ Jesus": no condemnation.

Not *"in Christ Jesus"*: no hope.

Given the options, you really want to be *"in Christ Jesus."* And the reason is because through Christ Jesus *"the law of the Spirit of life [sets] you free from the law of sin and death."*

By His sacrificial death on the Cross, Jesus took your place in the courtroom and paid the price for your sin. Jesus took on the condemnation you deserved.

In that process, your case was disconnected legally from the sin that got you into all your trouble with God. You were tried separately, and when God passed judgment, He passed judgment on sin—He condemned sin—without condemning you. When you went before God for your day in court, the death of Jesus was all your evidence and your only defense, and Jesus earned the pardon for your sins—a full pardon. Because of Jesus, despite your sins, *"there is now no condemnation"*—*if* you are *"in Christ Jesus."* There is no condemnation and never will be, even though you still sin and will continue to do so in this life.

❧

How is that possible?

---

[66] John 3:18, NIV.

Well, according to Paul, to be *"in Christ Jesus"*—and therefore to be exempt from condemnation for your sins—is to *"live according to the Spirit"*—capital "S"—the Holy Spirit—to have your mind set on what the Holy Spirit desires. It is to be controlled by the Holy Spirit, rather than by your human (and therefore sinful) instincts, impulses and desires.

This is not a one-time deal. It is not a baptism or a profession of faith or a confirmation, though it may start there. It is an ongoing, lifelong deal. It is living each day with God and toward God, instead of living without and away from God. It is trusting God continuously, because of Jesus Christ, by the power of the Holy Spirit in you.

If you are *"in Christ Jesus"*—if you are living according to the Holy Spirit within you—you are and always will be alive in the Spirit, free of the *condemnation* of sin from now on, just as you will be free from the *experience* of sin in eternity.

శ్రీ

So what do you do about your sins now—now that you know you will never face God's wrath and punishment for committing them?

Well, you may want to ignore them as though they don't matter. But don't do that. Even sins covered by the blood of Jesus Christ are displeasing to the God you will want with all your heart to please—if you are *"in Christ Jesus."*

But neither should you brood in anguish and shame over your sins and thus allow the devil a second victory by quenching the joy God has given you in giving you your full pardon for your sins.

Rather, confess your sins to God, knowing that *"He is faithful and just to forgive [your] sins and cleanse [you] from all unrighteousness."*[67]

And the admonition Jesus gave to the accusers of the woman caught in adultery—*"Let any one of you who is without sin be the first to*

---

[67] 1 John 1:9, RSV.

throw a stone at her"[68]—is just as appropriate for the woman herself. "Those who wanted to condemn you do not have the right; they are sinners, too. I do not condemn you. Do not condemn yourself. But go and sin no more."

"There is now no condemnation for those who are in Christ Jesus."

Instead, there is life in the Spirit. There is peace. There is hope. The verdict is in: full pardon. God's justice is rendered in your favor.

For you who are *"in Christ Jesus,"* God's court is adjourned. You will never be brought there again. You will never again be in jeopardy of God's judgment. Eternal condemnation is replaced with joyful communion—*"for those who are in Christ Jesus."*

ۻ“

---

[68] John 8:7, NIV.

Jeremiah 17:5-8 ESV

> [5] *Thus says the* LORD*:*
> *"Cursed is the man who trusts in man*
>   *and makes flesh his strength,*
>   *whose heart turns away from the* LORD*.*
> [6] *He is like a shrub in the desert,*
>   *and shall not see any good come.*
> *He shall dwell in the parched places of the wilderness,*
>   *in an uninhabited salt land.*
> [7] *"Blessed is the man who trusts in the* LORD*,*
>   *whose trust is the* LORD*.*
> [8] *He is like a tree planted by water,*
>   *that sends out its roots by the stream,*
> *and does not fear when heat comes,*
>   *for its leaves remain green,*
> *and is not anxious in the year of drought,*
>   *for it does not cease to bear fruit."*

ƎƜ

Romans 8:1-11 ESV

[1] *There is therefore now no condemnation for those who are in Christ Jesus.* [2] *For the law of the Spirit of life has set you free in Christ Jesus from the law of sin and death.* [3] *For God has done what the law, weakened by the flesh, could not do. By sending his own Son in the likeness of sinful flesh and for sin, he condemned sin in the flesh,* [4] *in order that the righteous requirement of the law might be fulfilled in us, who walk not according to the flesh but according to the Spirit.* [5] *For those who live according to the flesh set their minds on the things of the flesh, but those who live according to the Spirit set their minds on the things of the Spirit.* [6] *For to set the mind on the flesh is death, but to set the mind on the Spirit is life and peace.* [7] *For the mind that is set on the flesh is hostile to God, for it does not submit to God's law; indeed, it cannot.* [8] *Those who are in the flesh cannot please God.*

[9] *You, however, are not in the flesh but in the Spirit, if in fact the Spirit of God dwells in you. Anyone who does not have the Spirit of Christ does not belong to him.* [10] *But if Christ is in you, although the body is dead because of sin, the Spirit is life because of righteousness.* [11] *If the Spirit of him who raised Jesus from the dead dwells in you, he who raised Christ Jesus from the dead will also give life to your mortal bodies through his Spirit who dwells in you.*

৯◌৶

11.

One Way or the Other

Jeremiah 17:5-8; Romans 8:1-11 ESV

Everybody, every day, has to answer the same bedeviling question: "Which way?"

In everything we do or say, we're confronted with an option: "Which way?"

Even when there seems to be only one way—or no way—the question really won't go away: "Is this the right way—the best way—the only way?"

The truth is that even when there seem to be many ways—to live your life—to raise your family—to order your society—to strengthen your church—to sustain your nation—to secure your eternity—there are really only two. And, of those, only one actually works. Only one way "works."

The two ways—and here I would say, "of life"—except that only the one way that works is actually "of—life." The other "way of life" is not a way of life at all; it's a way of death.

But more about that in a minute....

❧

The two ways have gone by different names throughout history. Today, we often call them "the secular" and "the sacred."

75

There is the person who believes reality is limited to what may be labeled "the natural order." And there is the person who senses— and therefore submits and opens himself to—an additional and greater reality beyond what humanity can comprehend and control.

The Prophet Jeremiah called the two ways *"trusting in man"* and *"trusting in the Lord."* The Apostle Paul called them *"living according to the flesh"* and *"living according to the Spirit."*

And these are—always—the only two options you really have in life.

All the options that seem to be out there—all the nuances and variations and distinctions you may think you have chosen—they all boil down, in the end, to "with God" or "without God"—under God's authority, control and empowerment—or not.

And Jeremiah says that God says that "the secularist"— however distinct or diverse his variation—is cursed. Blessing is only available to the person who commits himself to the sacred— who trusts in God so completely that God actually *is* his trust.

And not just any God. We're talking about the God Who spoke through Jeremiah—and Paul—and in a unique way through Someone else I'll mention in a minute.

It seems rather harsh to say that people who choose to live secular lives are cursed. There are an awful lot of them—more and more all the time. And a lot of these people are our relatives and our friends. At one time—and perhaps not too long ago for some of us—they were us. But—hard as it seems—this is what the Bible says about them: "cursed."

∾

Now, having said that, I need to quibble with the translation we use in our 9:00 service[69] on one point. The *Good News Translation*

---

[69] This and many other of the sermons were preached three times (in three different services) on Sunday morning. The early service was a liturgical communion service based on the 1928 Episcopal Book of Common Prayer. The

renders the original Hebrew in verse 5 of Jeremiah 17 this way: *"The Lord says, 'I* **will condemn** *those who…put their trust in human beings…. '"*

It sounds like a threat—a promise of punishment: "I [God] will [actively] condemn!"

The translation we use in the other two services—the *English Standard Version*—has God stating a fact without threatening any action: *"those who put their trust…in human beings* **are cursed***."*

And that's a better translation.

❧

God doesn't have to do anything to those who have chosen to live without Him—or those who have tried to get Him to live with them on their own terms—for them to be cursed. They have cursed their own lives, themselves—without any help from God— because, as Jeremiah pictures it, they have "planted" themselves in a place that provides nothing to keep them nourished and alive.

Here's what you've got to understand: That "way" itself is cursed. This is not God issuing a threat. It's just God stating a universal and unalterable fact: The way of life without God—in whatever form it takes—is, by its very nature, a "god-less" way that leads to death rather than life—no matter how good or nice or important the person is who chooses it. The godless way is barren, for all its seeming beauty. It is as dry as death, for all its apparent appeal.

The man who trusts in man—in the ultimate sense—is cursed, and it doesn't matter if the "man" you trust in is you yourself, someone in your family, your military comrades, your social circle, your political party, your church or your country. Yes, we depend on others for many things, from trivial stuff to matters of great importance. And we seek to be dependable ourselves in fulfilling

---

second was a contemporary service using a modern version of the Bible. The third service was a more traditional Protestant service.

our obligations to others. And all that is well and good as far as it goes.

But when we do not put our trust in God—when we do not live according to the Spirit of God—everything we do or hope others will do for us is finally "a bust" because we remain cursed because it is God alone Who can give life. And God only gives life to those who have chosen to trust in Him and live according to the Spirit. And if God doesn't do what we need to have done, we're doomed.

But so many ways look so good.

The Proverbs say in more than one place: *"There is a way that seems right to a man, but its end is the way to death."*[70] That's the way that is other than God's way. That's the bad news—and it's truly awful.

చ•ళ

But here's the good news: *"There is now no condemnation for those who are in Christ Jesus. For the law of the Spirit of life in Christ Jesus has set me free from the law of sin and death."*

There *is* another way, other than the way that is cursed. *"Blessed is the man who trusts in the Lord"*—and let's be clear: we're not talking about "being spiritual" or "supporting the idea of religion" or "trying to be a good person." Paul means those who walk according to the Spirit and not the flesh—those whose minds are set on the Spirit and not on the things of the flesh. Jeremiah says the man who trusts in the Lord so completely and thoroughly that the Lord *is* his trust is blessed—like a tree that is going to flourish however hard the hardships get because its roots will get down deep in the kind of soil that never dries up no matter what the bad weather brings.

"There is a way that leads to life"—but only *one* way: total trust in God—Who has blessed our trust by bringing His Son Jesus Christ

---

[70] Proverbs 14:12; 16:24, RSV.

into our world—and Who blesses our lives even now by bringing His Son Jesus Christ into them.

ॐॐ

So, which way?
Sacred or secular?
Trusting God or trusting man?
With God—on His terms—or without Him, on any terms?
According to the Spirit or according to the flesh?
Blessed or cursed?
Life or death?
It's one way—or the other.

ॐॐ

Romans 8:14-17 NRSV

[14] *For all who are led by the Spirit of God are children of God.* [15] *For you did not receive a spirit of slavery to fall back into fear, but you have received a spirit of adoption. When we cry, "Abba! Father!"* [16] *it is that very Spirit bearing witness with our spirit that we are children of God,* [17] *and if children, then heirs, heirs of God and joint heirs with Christ—if, in fact, we suffer with him so that we may also be glorified with him.*

৯৽৽৽

12.

Led by the Spirit

Romans 8:14-17 NRSV

On Pentecost Sunday—today—we normally turn to Acts, Chapter 2, and marvel at the story of the pouring out of the Holy Spirit on the fragile, embryonic church in Jerusalem: a handful of people receiving a supernatural power to change the world.

And change it they did, for the passage we heard instead today was written only 20 to 25 years after that first Pentecost, by a man who hadn't been there, to a group of people a world away (in both miles and mindset) from Jerusalem, who had, nonetheless, experienced that same pouring out of the Spirit of God on them.

Those Christians in Rome *were* Christians—had experienced the coming of the Holy Spirit in their lives—because the Christians in Jerusalem had allowed themselves to be led by the Spirit they had received. The world changed, but the process didn't.

❧

Because the Christians in Jerusalem and Rome were led by the Spirit, you and I have heard the gospel, though we are another world away from both—again, in both miles and mindset.

And we here, on the basis of their testimony, and that of so many other Christians in between, have had the Holy Spirit poured out upon us, so that we, too, have been changed, and now possess the power to change the world.

We're not talking magic here, of course. We're talking about God, working out His will in the way He has chosen. We're talking about something Paul calls, *"being led by the Spirit."*

When the Holy Spirit was poured out upon the almost-but-not-quite-a-church in Jerusalem on Pentecost, it was divine power for the Church as a whole, but it was also divine power for every individual Christian. That's why Paul makes it personal.

ॐ

"All who are led by the Spirit are children of God," according to Paul. If you are led by the Spirit, you are a child of God. This is not about the *coming* of the Holy Spirit; it's about the *going* of the Holy Spirit. Pentecost is a remarkable historical event. Whole denominations have popped up based on the idea. But Paul's focus is on what the Holy Spirit was sent to do and whether you are getting on board with the Holy Spirit day by day.

To feel the Holy Spirit—to sense His presence and see the evidence of His power—to be enthused or even euphoric about the idea of the Holy Spirit—is not necessarily to be *led* by the Spirit. To be "led" implies that you will "follow."

Does the idea of being led by the Holy Spirit sound a little confining?

You certainly want to be comforted by the Holy Spirit. You want His spiritual protection from everything out there that threatens you. You wouldn't turn down the spiritual insight of the Holy Spirit, in theory at least. But to be *led* by the Holy Spirit is something else. Suppose the Holy Spirit decides to take you places you don't want to go.

When you are led by the Holy Spirit, you will run into a crowd—a crowd going the other way. It's only natural: You are going home to God your Father, and they are going round and round in circles, like water does going down the drain.

But you are a different story—if the Holy Spirit has been poured out on you and into you and you are following the Spirit as He leads you.

You are a different story if you're not trying to lead yourself through this life—if you're not depending on your own "spirituality" to design a spiritual process for yourself good enough that you don't have to bother actually following the Spirit when He leads.

෨෧

But Paul says, *"Everyone who is led by the Holy Spirit is a child of God."* He could have put it the other way around: "No one who is *not* led by the Holy Spirit is a child of God."

The Holy Spirit comes to you—to be your constant Companion. But He doesn't come to stay where you want Him to be. He comes to go where God wants *you* to be. It's Pentecost; the Holy Spirit has come: Time for children of God to follow the Leader.

෨෧

Romans 8:12-25 NRSV

[12] So then, brothers and sisters, we are debtors, not to the flesh, to live according to the flesh— [13] for if you live according to the flesh, you will die; but if by the Spirit you put to death the deeds of the body, you will live. [14] For all who are led by the Spirit of God are children of God. [15] For you did not receive a spirit of slavery to fall back into fear, but you have received a spirit of adoption. When we cry, "Abba! Father!" [16] it is that very Spirit bearing witness with our spirit that we are children of God, [17] and if children, then heirs, heirs of God and joint heirs with Christ—if, in fact, we suffer with him so that we may also be glorified with him.

[18] I consider that the sufferings of this present time are not worth comparing with the glory about to be revealed to us. [19] For the creation waits with eager longing for the revealing of the children of God; [20] for the creation was subjected to futility, not of its own will but by the will of the one who subjected it, in hope [21] that the creation itself will be set free from its bondage to decay and will obtain the freedom of the glory of the children of God. [22] We know that the whole creation has been groaning in labor pains until now; [23] and not only the creation, but we ourselves, who have the first fruits of the Spirit, groan inwardly while we wait for adoption, the redemption of our bodies. [24] For in hope we were saved. Now hope that is seen is not hope. For who hopes for what is seen? [25] But if we hope for what we do not see, we wait for it with patience.

੩∘৯

13.

Suffering with Christ

Romans 8:12-25 NRSV

Over the next few months, you will see an interesting technology demonstrated on TV as part of the political campaigns. Pollsters are now able to have people register on a handheld machine their reaction to what a candidate is saying as he or she is saying it. You can see a group change from approval to disapproval and back again as different things are said.

If this technology had been available in Rome when Paul's letter was read to the Christians there, you likely would have seen a high approval rating when he said they were *"children of God"* and *"fellow heirs with Christ."* But I imagine the part about *"suffering with Christ"* would have sent the indicator quickly into negative territory.

Paul says the suffering that a Christian shares with Christ in the present—in this world—is nothing compared to the glory the Christian will share with Christ in eternity. But the suffering comes first—and without the suffering: no glory.

Glory is a winning concept, but suffering is never going to be popular, even when it is linked to glory.

Many people—some of them Christians—seem to think (or live as though) these two things aren't linked, or don't have to be: "I'll have a double helping of glory, please, but hold the suffering."

We'd all like the benefits of salvation without the burdens of the Christian life. We'd like our religious experience to be convenient, comfortable and compatible with our other commitments. But Jesus says, "If you would be My disciple, take up your cross and follow Me."[71] Sounds rather un-comfortable and in-convenient. No wonder everybody's not rushing to join up.

After all, who but a fool—or masochist—wants to suffer? Jesus Himself did not want to suffer.[72] And His Church is not made up of masochists. But Jesus did choose to suffer—for a reason.[73] And He requires His disciples to suffer for the same reason.

Only a fool wants to suffer. But pity the poor wretch who doesn't want something in life—or beyond—that he is willing to suffer to obtain. If we were not willing to suffer for something, every gymnasium would close tomorrow, heroism would be non-existent, and brute force would rule in every situation.

Jesus Christ chose to suffer for a reason, and Christians have chosen to believe in that reason and suffer with Christ for it as a result. But before we talk about the reason, we need to make a distinction about suffering.

ॐ✦

There are actually two kinds of suffering. One could be called "natural" suffering: what everybody experiences as a natural consequence of this being a fallen and corrupt world. As the old cliché puts it so quaintly: "Into every life a little rain must fall"[74]—except that, from time to time, the bottom falls out: flood and fire, disease and death. Everybody suffers in this world, saint and scoundrel alike.

---

[71] Mark 8:34.

[72] Matthew 26:39.

[73] Hebrews 12:2; Romans 14:15; 1 Peter 3:18.

[74] It turns out I slightly misquoted the next to last line from Henry Wadsworth Longfellow's poem, "Rainy Day," published in 1842. The correct wording is "Into each life some rain must fall."

We make our natural suffering worse, of course, by sinful actions and attitudes—by selfishness and greed, suspicion and malice, skewed values, poor judgment and addictions of all kinds. To live is to suffer. To live foolishly is to suffer more. That's just the way it is in this world.

But there is another kind of suffering: the suffering of Christ. This is a redemptive suffering. In a way, it is voluntary suffering— suffering that doesn't have to be. It is what happened when Jesus Christ chose to obey God, Who sent Him to break sin's chokehold on the world. The world, at sin's direction, fought back—to the death, in fact. But before it got Jesus to the Cross, the world was already attacking Him, morally, intellectually and socially.

Though He could have avoided the suffering the world inflicted on Him (by giving up the quest of salvation and blending back into the helpless and hopeless mass of humanity around Him), Jesus chose to endure great suffering in order to do the work God sent Him to do: to evict—by force—the evil controlling the world—by the force of His suffering love for those under the control of that evil.

৯৯৩

Some choose to accept the work of Jesus rather than oppose it. Some accept His salvation from this painful existence. They line up with Him against a world He means to save. And whatever the world throws at Jesus is going to splatter on them because they have chosen to be close to Him—next to Him.

These people will inherit the glory that awaits Jesus for defeating sin and transforming all of Creation. And the glory will be appropriate, in quantity and quality, to the achievement.

You cannot earn your own salvation, no matter how much you suffer for the cause of Christ. But your willingness to suffer with Christ and for Christ is a clear indication that you have believed the gospel and committed yourself to the One Whose suffering was sufficient to save you. Your suffering with Christ is your greatest testimony *to* Christ and service *for* Christ.

If you claim Christ as your Savior, you've become a child of God and an heir with Christ. Full-fledged children—heirs—inherit exactly what the only begotten Son inherits, which, in this case, is suffering for righteousness' sake in this world, and glory—unimaginable, inexpressible glory—in the next.

Perhaps that's why Jesus said, *"Blessed are those who are persecuted for righteousness' sake, for theirs is the kingdom of heaven. Blessed are you when men revile you and persecute you and utter all kinds of evil against you falsely on my account. Rejoice and be glad, for your reward is great in heaven."*[75]

Or as Paul put it: *"We suffer with him in order that we may also be glorified with him."*

You won't get much credit or benefit in this world for suffering with Christ—this world is inflicting the suffering, after all.

But God sees and knows what you suffer for Christ and with Christ, and God is—first, last and always—a generous Father to His obedient children—willing and able to reward them beyond their wildest imaginations—to provide an eternal reward that is nothing short of glorious.

I can hardly wait.

❧

---

[75] Matthew 5:10-12, RSV.

Romans 8:26-39 NRSV

 [26] *Likewise the Spirit helps us in our weakness; for we do not know how to pray as we ought, but that very Spirit intercedes with sighs too deep for words.*
 [27] *And God, who searches the heart, knows what is the mind of the Spirit, because the Spirit intercedes for the saints according to the will of God.*
 [28] *We know that all things work together for good for those who love God, who are called according to his purpose.* [29] *For those whom he foreknew he also predestined to be conformed to the image of his Son, in order that he might be the firstborn within a large family.* [30] *And those whom he predestined he also called; and those whom he called he also justified; and those whom he justified he also glorified.*
 [31] *What then are we to say about these things? If God is for us, who is against us?* [32] *He who did not withhold his own Son, but gave him up for all of us, will he not with him also give us everything else?* [33] *Who will bring any charge against God's elect? It is God who justifies.* [34] *Who is to condemn? It is Christ Jesus, who died, yes, who was raised, who is at the right hand of God, who indeed intercedes for us.* [35] *Who will separate us from the love of Christ? Will hardship, or distress, or persecution, or famine, or nakedness, or peril, or sword?* [36] *As it is written,*

> *"For your sake we are being killed all day long;*
> *we are accounted as sheep to be slaughtered."*

 [37] *No, in all these things we are more than conquerors through him who loved us.* [38] *For I am convinced that neither death, nor life, nor angels, nor rulers, nor things present, nor things to come, nor powers,* [39] *nor height, nor depth, nor anything else in all creation, will be able to separate us from the love of God in Christ Jesus our Lord.*

৵◌৻

14.

A Sure Thing

Romans 8:26-39 NRSV

The story is told about Queen Maria Theresa of Austria that when she was very old and very ill, she lay in bed, fading in and out of consciousness. The clergy, then as now, had been summoned and one man of the cloth, in trying to offer what comfort he could to her and those attending her, intoned in a voice of reverent piety, "The only sure and certain thing in life is death." To which the wizened old women responded in a faint but firm whisper, "…and taxes."[76]

Either way, there don't seem to be many sure things in life—and certainly not many good ones. People who want to offer you a "hot tip" on a "sure thing" should generally be avoided.

But there are a number of things every Christian may depend on with absolute, blessed assurance. The New Testament is full of them, in fact, and some of the most important "sure things" are found in Romans 8—in the verses that conclude the chapter: "…*neither death, nor life, nor angels, nor things present, nor things to come,*

---

[76] I cannot find my source for this story, and further research suggests that it is fiction. Most sources attribute the saying to Benjamin Franklin in a 1789 letter, or the general idea to Daniel Defoe's *The Political History of the Devil*, 1726.

nor powers, nor height, nor depth, nor anything else in all creation, will be able to separate us from the love of God in Christ Jesus our Lord."

It's a sure thing.

"He who did not withhold his own Son, but gave him up for all of us, will he not with him also give us everything else?"

It's a sure thing.

Even verse 28—where the translation you heard offers an unfortunate translation of the Greek—contains an amazing assertion which should be rendered: *"...in all things, God works for good with those who love him and are called according to his purpose."*

God is redeeming everything.

It's another sure thing.

The certainty of death and taxes are easy to believe. God's unlimited provision, undeterred redemption, and un-lose-able love may be less so, because these latter realities flow over into the supernatural and eternal. But the hardest sure thing to believe in may be the amazing promise about prayer in verses 26 and 27: *"...the Spirit helps us in our weakness; for we do not know how to pray as we ought, but the Spirit himself intercedes for us with sighs too deep for words. And he who searches the hearts of men knows what is the mind of the Spirit, because the Spirit intercedes for the saints* (that's you and me) *according to the will of God."*

৵৽৽

Or to put it more simply, when you pray as a Christian, it's a sure thing. That's very hard to believe, because many of us are very frustrated with our prayer life—even embarrassed by it. It feels like—looks to us like—anything but a sure thing.

"I don't feel like my prayers go anywhere!"

Fortunately, it's not about how you *feel*; it's about what you *know* because it has been revealed to you.

And what does it matter if your prayers don't get beyond the ceiling? Remember that the intercessory activity of the Holy Spirit takes over whenever your own ability to pray falls short. The Holy Spirit intercedes and carries your prayers directly to God.

It's like being in a free-throw contest, and when it's your turn, you get to toss the ball to someone like Michael Jordan to shoot the basket for you. The only difference is that when you toss your prayers at the Holy Spirit, He *never* misses. *Every* prayer you give to the Holy Spirit to "shoot up" to God, scores. Or, to continue the sports analogies, it's like a Home Run Derby where you let Babe Ruth take your cuts, except that *every* swipe the Holy Spirit takes at the "prayer ball" is a home run.

The result of your prayer is not the result of your ability to pray, but of the Holy Spirit's ability to intercede. And the Holy Spirit is more persuasive that any big trial lawyer's silver-tongued appeal to any judge.

Oh, and by the way, the Holy Spirit has an "in" with the Judge. They're like two minds thinking as one—all the time. The Judge of all the world listens to *everything* this Advocate has to say—on your behalf.

"But I don't know how to pray!"

Who does? And so what?

Does a mother get frustrated with her baby because he can't speak in complete and cogent sentences? What does she do when her baby babbles gibberish at her? She repeats the gibberish back to the baby with delight. She interacts with him at his level. She teaches her baby to speak by responding to whatever he offers her, enjoying the mere fact that her child is trying to communicate with her.

And you know what else, most of the time the mother knows what the baby is "saying" even though he can't form any understandable words. She understands because he's her baby and she's paying attention to his every action and mood. It's not the words—it's the relationship. It's not what he says that pleases her, since he can't "say" anything that *would* please her. It's his desire to interact with her that delights her, even though he isn't mature enough to say anything that would engage or challenge the mother on an intellectual level.

And what's the difference between this earthly mother and our Heavenly Father?

Most of the time, the mother *mostly* knows what's going on with her baby. God, our Heavenly Father, *always* knows *all* that is going on inside your head—and your heart. He always knows what you're trying to say.

જ~৫

Then why do we concern ourselves at all about the content of our prayers? Why do we read prayers as acts of devotion or recite prayers together as part of public worship? Why does the Bible record so many prayers—from beginning to end? Why did Jesus teach His disciples to pray?[77]

The words of these prayers that are carefully composed and ceremoniously shared and painstakingly preserved are for you, not for God. Jesus taught His disciples to pray, not so that God would hear better, more eloquent and theologically satisfying prayers, but so that the disciples would grow in faith and perception and be refined spiritually as they thought more maturely about the things of God and the nature of God and the will of God for them.

Have you not experienced greater hope and new insight and deeper commitment and renewed strength and richer joy in the very act of prayer? Do not the words of great and common prayers bless and inspire you?

It is the Holy Spirit helping you in your weakness, perfecting your prayers to God and providing for your needs in the very act of your praying, however feeble and inadequate your efforts may seem to be (to you).

God has poured out His Holy Spirit on all believers and the Spirit helps us in our weakness, interceding for us—speaking for

---

[77] Luke 11:1-4.

us to God in a language beyond our capacity to understand, in prayers so deep and profound that we could not begin to appreciate their truth or beauty or power to satisfy God and motivate God to act for our benefit—if He needed motivation, which He does not.

The power or success of your prayers does not depend on you—thank God!—but on God Himself. You are weak. He is strong. You start and He will finish.

ॐ◦⊛

If God has given you a spectacular weapon to ensure your success in the spiritual warfare of this life, and the enemy can't take it away from you, this enemy's only hope is to suggest to you that it doesn't work or is too complicated for you to use. The only hope the enemy has is to undermine your confidence in the undefeatable equipment you've been given so that you don't use it to attain the victory that is certain if you do. You must not be deceived by the enemy's propaganda.

Our salvation makes us a part of God's vast army of redemption, serving the cause of Christ in restoring all of Creation. And if we know anything about prayer on the personal level, this new "theatre of operations" on the cosmic scale is certainly beyond us.

We don't know how to pray in the face of the cosmic complexity God has involved us in. But that's okay: The Holy Spirit helps us in our weakness. All we have to do is "pull the trigger" on prayer and fire away. "Higher Headquarters" will do the rest. When we pray with the help of the Holy Spirit, every prayer is on target.

We do not know how to pray as we ought, but we do not need to be concerned about this. There is Someone Who does know how to pray and will do so for us.

Do you remember the scene from the end of the movie *Close Encounters of the Third Kind*,[78] when all those who had been led to the mountain top by some powerful and mysterious entity, gathered in the hope of communicating with someone who seemed totally alien to them? In the midst of them stood one pathetic, geeky-looking fellow at a keyboard, terrified yet determined to play a few notes, to repeat the simple tune this great power had taught him. He stands in awe before something that he cannot begin to fathom and does what little he can.

Help us out, John.[79]

৵৽

That's right. That's all the fellow in the movie knows how to do. He plays his few notes—and then, he plays them again. Then the mysterious "other" responds—answers—and even though the fellow does not know what the answer means, they have made contact.

And then, after he has played the notes he knows, engaging at his painfully primitive level, he takes his fingers off the keys and lets a more powerful mind take over the music making. And then, the real interaction begins.

"God is great. God is good. Let us thank Him for our food...."
[I PRETEND TO PLAY NOTES WITH BOTH HANDS
ON AN IMAGINARY KEYBOARD,
AND THEN LIFT MY FINGERS.]

"Now I lay me down to sleep, I pray the Lord my soul to keep...."
[AGAIN, I "PLAY NOTES"
AND LIFT MY HANDS]

---

[78] Movie, *Close Encounters of the Third Kind*, 1977.

[79] John Shannon, our very talented organist, played (by prior arrangement) the famous five-note theme from the movie on the Chapel's massive pipe organ.

"Our Father Who art in heaven, hallowed be Thy name...."
　　　[I "PLAY NOTES" AGAIN,
　　　　AND LIFT MY HANDS.]

"Help me, Jesus!"
　　　　[I "PLAY NOTES" STILL AGAIN,
　　　　　AND LIFT MY HANDS.]

Simple tunes.
A baby's gibberish.
A believer's prayer.
And the Spirit's intercession....
　　[THIS TIME, I "HOLD THE NOTES" LONGER
　　　BEFORE LIFTING MY HANDS.]

Pray!
It's a sure thing.

☙❧

Romans 8:26-39 ESV

[26] *Likewise the Spirit helps us in our weakness. For we do not know what to pray for as we ought, but the Spirit himself intercedes for us with groanings too deep for words.* [27] *And he who searches hearts knows what is the mind of the Spirit, because the Spirit intercedes for the saints according to the will of God.* [28] *And we know that for those who love God all things work together for good, for those who are called according to his purpose.* [29] *For those whom he foreknew he also predestined to be conformed to the image of his Son, in order that he might be the firstborn among many brothers.* [30] *And those whom he predestined he also called, and those whom he called he also justified, and those whom he justified he also glorified.*

[31] *What then shall we say to these things? If God is for us, who can be against us?* [32] *He who did not spare his own Son but gave him up for us all, how will he not also with him graciously give us all things?* [33] *Who shall bring any charge against God's elect? It is God who justifies.* [34] *Who is to condemn? Christ Jesus is the one who died—more than that, who was raised—who is at the right hand of God, who indeed is interceding for us.* [35] *Who shall separate us from the love of Christ? Shall tribulation, or distress, or persecution, or famine, or nakedness, or danger, or sword?* [36] *As it is written,*

> *"For your sake we are being killed all the day long;*
> *we are regarded as sheep to be slaughtered."*

[37] *No, in all these things we are more than conquerors through him who loved us.* [38] *For I am sure that neither death nor life, nor angels nor rulers, nor things present nor things to come, nor powers,* [39] *nor height nor depth, nor anything else in all creation, will be able to separate us from the love of God in Christ Jesus our Lord.*

৵•ৎ

15.

In All Things, God

Romans 8:26-39 ESV

Most of us know the "story" of our lives by heart. This happened and then that. This was good. That was bad. We know where we've been and what we've done—and what's been done to us.

And the Apostle Paul says we know something else: "We know that in all things, God is collaborating with those who love Him to cause good to result."

"In all things, God...." In all the great turning points in history—in all the decisive battles and key elections—in every natural disaster and every marvelous medical advance—God has been there, working for good. And in your life—in the events that formed your identity and your perspective—that turn up in every narrative you tell about yourself—or would tell, if you were the type to tell your life's story—God has been there, working for good, regardless of whether what He had to work with was good or bad.

Paul says Christians know this. I hope you do. But maybe you don't know it as well as you think you do—as well as you should.

Let's find out.

Paul is *not* saying, for instance, that "everything works out for the best." In fact, everything *doesn't* work out for the best. This is a fallen, broken, sinful world. A lot of bad things happen.

Some of them have happened to you. More of them will. It's that kind of world. Left to its own devices, the world isn't going to do much good. The same is true for people—left to their own devices.

What Paul is saying is that God is not leaving the world to its own devices. God is "interactive." God is so interactive that nothing gets by Him un-acted upon. You could go home today and take every story in the newspaper and write on it: "In this, God is working—and will continue to be working— for good," and there would be more truth in what you wrote *on* the paper than anything written *in* the paper—whatever the story.

You can do the same for everything that has ever happened in your life. Take the most wonderful thing that ever happened to you. In addition to all the joy, or satisfaction, or benefit you derived from the thing itself, God was also working in it for a special divine kind of good.

Take the worst things that have happened to you—things that have broken your heart and wrecked your life—that haunt you to this day. Even in these—perhaps especially in these—God is now, and has always been, working for good.

And in every little thing of such insignificance that you forgot it as soon as it happened?

God has been working in all these, too—for good. God has been busy, and will remain so, because He has no plans to change His process or His purpose. In everything—absolutely everything—God is working for good. The world is not working for good. "Everything" is not working for good. *God* is working for good.

And according to Paul, God is not working alone.

☙❧

The Greek word Paul uses for what God is doing is συνεργεῖ—
"synergy." It means working with somebody—collaborating—
"co-laboring." It's not just that God is working for good—as
wonderful as that is.

God has help.

Now it's not a lot of help, in comparison to what God is doing.
It's kind of like me helping the workman who shows up at my
house. I help him by letting him in my house when he knocks and
showing him to the place where something needs to be installed or
repaired. I help by being available for whatever he wants of me
without trying to tell him how to do a job he knows how to do far
better than I do.

Who is God's helper? Who is the one that God has chosen to
"work together with" to bring good out of everything?

Paul refers to *"those who love God and are called according to God's
purpose"*—or more accurately: *"the ones who **are loving** God and **are
being called...**"*—those who are actively engaged in an ongoing
relationship with God marked by their actively loving God and
continuously experiencing God's claim on their lives—God's call
to join Him in His redemptive work.

It's like a mother who invites a little daughter to "help her
cook," or a father who invites a young son to help him build
something in the garage. In neither case is the beloved child an
equal partner in the process. The child is not necessary at all, except
that the doting parent wants the "help," delighting to have the child
sharing in the project.

In the same way, God has chosen to partner with us—to let us
help Him cause good to come out of everything.

Of course, if Mother is making meat loaf for dinner and her
little helper is only willing to make mud pies, cooking won't seem
good to the daughter. And if Daddy's helper wants to hammer the
side of the car instead of the nails in the birdhouse, there won't be
much productive collaboration from the youngster's perspective.

But if the child wants to do whatever it is the parent is doing because he or she loves the parent, then it's a different story.

And as we are loving our Heavenly Father and accepting His calling on our lives, we will see that everything God does with us, and for us, is good.

And how do we know that all this is so? How do we know that God really does make good come out of everything, especially the truly bad things?

ॐ∽ॐ

We start with the worst thing of all: the Crucifixion of the only begotten Son of God.

Perfect innocence and totally selfless love were destroyed by the ultimate expression of evil. And even in that, God was working with His Son—collaborating with Him to bring the ultimate good out of that ultimate evil, which is what God did in the Resurrection of Jesus on Easter morning. The devil did his worst and God responded with His best, and the process has continued in that way ever since.

And for the early Christians—and far too many of their modern counterparts—the trouble, hardship, persecution, famine, nakedness, peril and sword Paul refers to are far too real.

Yet in the suffering they endured and are enduring, God has established and strengthened the Church and transformed countless lives.

In the loss of your loved ones, or the onset of grave illness, or the shattering of some dream, God is working with you, even now, to take the agony and transform it into something that blesses someone—you or someone else—and brings God's ultimate purpose of redemption a little closer to its consummation.

ॐ∽ॐ

But let's be clear. Even in doing all the good He does—even though you love Him and are called according to His purpose, God does not spare you from suffering. Sometimes, if you live according to your calling, and return God's love for you with all your heart, you will avoid some of life's pain or sorrow. God's way is a good way, and far better than the world's way. Obedience is better than rebellion, though it may take living in obedience over time to see the greatest benefits.

But Christians will suffer—sometimes for their faith and sometimes just as part of a common humanity. And whatever the cause of suffering, you are to know that God is injecting Himself into every situation—every sorrow, every disappointment, every difficulty—to cause redemption—to transform the suffering—and you—for the good. God is working with you—in all things—for good.

༼ঌ•ঌ༽

But suppose you can't see it.

You don't have to see it—if you know it to be so. And Paul says, "We know it; we know it is so." You will not always see God's redemptive good being worked out—and certainly not in the heat or heartbreak of the moment.

But that's why you have to know it—that's why you have to look back at other times and situations and see now that God was there, working to bless the good and redeem the evil and the painful.

What you can't see now, you know you *will* see. You know you will see *every* situation redeemed by the God Who loves you and calls you—and redeems you and everything about your life as a measure of Who He is.

"But I don't see it!"

But you will!

༼ঌ•ঌ༽

I don't mean to say that every financial reversal will be followed by a winning lottery ticket delivered in the mail—or dropped directly out of heaven. And sometimes they're right that "no good deed goes unpunished."

But God never lets it go. God never accepts the wrong of sin or the pain of suffering. God never lets the devil get away with it. God is transforming everything—touching everything for good in collaboration with us.

And don't be surprised if the transforming and redeeming is not about *your* comfort or restoration. God may be using your pain—your suffering—to heal someone else's wounds. What Paul is really saying is that if you love God and having submitted yourself to God's purpose—which is the redemption of Creation and everything in it—you will be pleased with what you and God are doing together.

If you know that God is redeeming everything—that God is actively engaged in everything with whoever is loving Him and submitting to Him—what are we to say about what we have gone through and what we are going through, even now?

We say, "We know that everything—good and bad—will end up good because God is actively working it out that way." We're helping where God seems to want us to. And others like us are doing the same thing—in some cases, to our direct benefit, because that's what God is letting them help Him do.

And so we worship God, not just because of the wonderful blessings we receive from His involvement in our lives, but because of our opportunity to share in the redemptive activity of God that blesses and sustains others.

In every thing, God....

In all things, God....

In your life, God....

In the lives of other Christians, God....

In every situation in this world requiring the redemptive grace of God, God....

Now and for all eternity, God is working with us—working for us—calling us to be His—and loving us enough for us to be able to love Him back, so that we can love what He's doing and recognize it for the infinite and wonderful good that it is.

In all things, God is working with us for good.

You knew this, right?

If you didn't, you do now.

❧

Romans 8:35-39 RSV

[35] *Who shall separate us from the love of Christ? Shall tribulation, or distress, or persecution, or famine, or nakedness, or peril, or sword?* [36] *As it is written,*

> *"For thy sake we are being killed all the day long;*
> *we are regarded as sheep to be slaughtered."*

[37] *No, in all these things we are more than conquerors through him who loved us.* [38] *For I am sure that neither death, nor life, nor angels, nor principalities, nor things present, nor things to come, nor powers,* [39] *nor height, nor depth, nor anything else in all creation, will be able to separate us from the love of God in Christ Jesus our Lord.*

ॐ

16.

America and God after "9/11"

Romans 8:35-39 RSV

At 9:37 on that sunny autumn morning, American Airlines Flight 77 roared over the roof of the Navy Annex where I was assigned. Seconds later, it plunged into the side of the Pentagon nearby. Windows in our building rattled as the plane passed yards above and people watched in horror as it exploded into the Pentagon and sent a massive fireball skyward. The shockwave from the impact then shook the Annex again.

There were a lot of chaplains in the Pentagon that morning—many more than usual. Senior chaplains of all services had come from around the world for a conference. When the plane hit, they ran to evacuate the injured, seek out the missing, and minister to thousands in shock, confusion, fear, and grief.

They were soon joined by other chaplains who raced down the hill from the Annex. Throughout the day, these chaplains and more moved among the crowds, comforting, consoling, encouraging and praying with those who had just survived an unimaginable evil.

At the same time, other people were working feverishly to account for tens of thousands of people who were (or might have been) in the Pentagon when the plane hit: "Who was in there? Who wasn't? And what happened to those who were?"

By late afternoon, a list of the missing—the unaccounted for—had taken shape. That evening, the task of notifying families began. Dozens of chaplains joined notification officers and unit representatives to fan out across northern Virginia, southern Maryland, and the District of Columbia—to make the dreaded calls.

My group knocked on a door at midnight and found a young wife and two sets of parents. We told them what they already knew: "He's missing. They're searching around the clock. Tomorrow, we hope…."

"He just graduated from Annapolis," they told us, "His brother was a Navy flyer who died in a flight deck crash two years ago."

We prayed together and left them in the wee hours of the morning.

His remains were identified several days later. His chaplain from the Naval Academy conducted his funeral at Arlington National Cemetery.

శ్రీల

In the days and weeks that followed, we ministered to the survivors. We shared the grief and anger of a nation. And we sought to make sense of the senseless.

A year has passed. Day by day, the flood of feelings that washed over us and carried us along in those early days has receded as the normal currents of our lives returned. Time heals. And we survived.

But what have we learned?

What did we learn by watching helplessly as maniacs we do not know slipped into our nation and our neighborhood to slaughter thousands of innocent men, women, and children, to destroy great symbols of cooperative endeavor, to rend the fabric of a free and peaceful society, and then to escape into the dark sanctuary of death?

What do we learn from the news that others like them are still planning and preparing to do the same—and worse—to us, and may succeed, despite our best efforts to prevent them?

You may think: "There is nothing to be learned from something as demonic as this!"

But I think there is much to learn, and we may, in fact, learn best from our suffering. The most important lessons I have learned relate to the value of America, and to its limitations, and to the all-sufficiency of the God revealed in Jesus Christ.

෨෬

I pledge allegiance to the flag of the United States of America and to the republic for which it stands.[80]

I do solemnly swear to support and defend the Constitution of the United States against all enemies foreign and domestic.[81]

I wear the uniform of the military forces of my country and have served at the pleasure of half a dozen presidents.

September 11, 2001, found me already—by choice and by inclination—a loyal and patriotic American.

But the savage events of that day and the diverse reactions to them around the world—and even within our own borders—have caused me to reexamine the place and purpose of America—in the world and in my life.

I remain absolutely convinced that America is a miraculous gift of God. It is not the new Israel, or the kingdom of God on earth.

But, at the same time, it is too unlikely to be an accident, and too wonderful to be our own doing.

This past summer, my wife and I drove from Washington, D.C., to Mount Rushmore. The reason for the trip—and for *driving*

---

[80] The first line of The Pledge of Allegiance.
[81] The first line of the Oath of Office members of the American military swear upon entering service, reenlisting and being promoted.

it—was to see for ourselves the spacious skies, waves of grain, majestic mountains, and fruited plains we always sing about.[82] And we found them all, in breathtaking splendor and abundance.

All the terrorists in the world—all doing their destructive worst—could not greatly diminish the God-created natural grandeur we enjoy in America. The land is just too big and too strong and too beautiful. We are above all a people most fortunate to be living our lives in this remarkable place. America is of immeasurable value to me as a place, a country.

⮞⮜

But America is more—so very much more—than just a land that stretches from "sea to shining sea."[83] America is the promise of "liberty and justice for all."[84] It is the dedication (of a vast multitude of remarkably diverse people) "to the proposition that all men are created equal."[85] America is an amazing idea, a noble experiment, a glorious vision of how imperfect people can live together in peace and prosperity.

Surely no nation in history has provided such opportunity for both personal freedom and quality of life to all its citizens. And just as surely, no nation in history has given so much and been of such positive benefit to the other nations of the world. America's very existence proclaims the vision of our blessing, and protects the possibility that others may someday experience it for themselves.

Those who would subject the people of the world to their inhumane control must first block the light of freedom and hope that shines so brightly in us and from us to those sorely oppressed. The determination of our enemies to attack us, to knock down our

---

[82] Katherine Lee Bates, "America the Beautiful," 1895. The music was written by Samuel A. Ward in 1910.
[83] From "America the Beautiful."
[84] From The Pledge of Allegiance.
[85] From *The Gettysburg Address*, by Abraham Lincoln, November 16, 1863.

towers (and by doing so to cripple our inspiring American influence), is actually their twisted acknowledgement of America's great and enduring value to the world.

And things of great value require and deserve great effort and great sacrifice for their protection. So thought the passengers of United Flight 93 when they took their lives back from the hijackers and then sacrificed them over Shanksville, Pennsylvania, to protect their fellow citizens and the cherished symbols of America.

In the same way, firemen, and policemen and others protected the American idea from the terrorist assault by giving their lives for strangers whose lives the murderers were determined to take.

And our armed forces show America's tremendous value today, taking battle to the enemy's back yard, not just to inflict revenge, or even to prevent more attacks, but to secure the blessings of an American-type liberty for even the most severely oppressed in those faraway places. I have learned anew, from the suffering that came on and after September 11th, the incalculable value of America.

❧

But I have also learned something of America's limitations. The destruction of lives and property in New York, Washington, and Pennsylvania destroyed the illusion of American invulnerability as well. For all our military power, America cannot guarantee that you and I will not die an untimely death. America cannot guarantee that we will not be the innocent victims of vicious enemies. As the concrete and steel came crashing down, so, too, did our illusions that America was somehow magic, like a force field of protection around us.

No longer can we think we know what tomorrow holds in store for us, or that tomorrow holds only the fulfillment of our dreams because, after all, *"This is America!"*

America will survive—if we serve her best interests and protect her from the harm others would do her. And I believe God would have us do just that. But there is no guarantee that preserving America will not require more *from* us than it will provide *to* us, whether in life, liberty, property, or happiness.

To say this is not to criticize America. In this, America has not failed. We have simply learned how vulnerable we really are in this life, even living in America. What September 11th has done is to dispel some dangerous illusions about America that were possible and easy to hold because of how wonderful our nation is. America gives us so much that we are tempted to expect it to give us everything. It can do so much, why shouldn't it be able to do all things for all people? Pass a law. Issue an order. Write a check.

But we learned in a classroom of fire and death that though America is, in a sense, a beacon of hope and possibility, it is not "the Light of the world." September 11th taught us to recognize more clearly the difference between America and God.

৵৵

Now we find ourselves at the mercy of evil men plotting our physical destruction. But—hallelujah!—we also find ourselves within the grace of a loving and powerful God Who has already provided for our spiritual salvation. As we remember those lost on September 11th—and on the battlefields that terror has spawned around the world—as we give thanks for, and renew our commitment to, America and all the positive things America represents—we still find that it is God alone Who provides the ultimate security, because only God can offer an eternal security. Only God is able to keep us from falling when our world is crashing down around us.

America's finest warriors have gone to some of the most challenging places in the world. They are defeating some of our deadliest enemies. Their success has been impressive, but limited. Yet there is no place—in this world or the next—where the eye of God cannot see, and the hand of God cannot reach. And no one will escape God's judgment.

We *know* the gospel; we've known it for a long time. Now we *need* it like we've never needed it before. We can save America from terrorists, and should, but America cannot "save" us, in this world or the next. Only God can—and He will, if we *believe* the gospel we know.

࿔

Admiral Tim Ziemer, now retired, grew up in South Vietnam in the '50s and '60s, the child of Presbyterian missionaries. He tells of "knowing" the gospel because he grew up with parents who taught it to him and lived it before him.

But as a child, he only *knew* it. When the time came, he returned to the United States to go to a Christian college, *knowing* the gospel, but not yet seeing a need to *believe* it.

Then one day, he got word that his parents had been trapped in the fierce fighting at Khe Sanh.[86] His father had approached the North Vietnamese under a flag of truce to negotiate the evacuation of noncombatants and had been executed for his efforts. His mother had been badly wounded and captured during one of the attacks shortly after. Then, assuming she would die, the Communists threw her off the back of a truck into a ditch when they were forced to retreat.

But she did not die. She was found and treated and flown to the United States with wounded soldiers from the siege.

So here he was, a young man in college: one godly parent murdered; the other terribly wounded. Tim Ziemer realized in his shock and grief and anger that now he had to decide whether he would finally *believe* the gospel he had merely *known* all his life. When his wonderful world fell apart, he realized his only hope was to *believe* in the God of the gospel, the God and Father of our Lord Jesus Christ.

---

[86] The Battle of Khe Sanh lasted from January 21st to July 9th of 1968. Two or three divisions of the North Vietnamese army attacked the base defended by two regiments of American Marines.

That decision made, he went to meet his mother when her hospital plane landed, wondering how she could possibly survive her pain and her loss—wondering what he should say to her.

Still confined to her bed, her wounds too severe to permit speech, his mother took a note pad when she saw him board the plane and she began to write as he walked down the aisle toward her.

When she finished writing, she handed him the pad and Tim Ziemer read these words:

> "When upon life's billows you are tempest tossed,
> When you are discouraged, thinking all is lost,
> Count your many blessings; name them one by one,
> And it will surprise you what the Lord has done."[87]

Mrs. Ziemer had learned long before to believe the gospel—to trust in the all-sufficient God—and God had been sufficient for all her needs.

ॐ

The Apostle Paul wrote, *"I consider that the sufferings of this present time are not worth comparing with the glory that is to be revealed to us."*[88]

The Apostle Paul wrote, *"Who shall separate us from the love of Christ? Shall tribulation, or distress, or persecution, or famine, or nakedness, or peril, or sword? Even as it is written,*

> *'For thy sake we are killed all the day long;*
> *We are regarded as sheep for the slaughter.*

No, in all these things we are more than conquerors through him that loved us.

For I am persuaded, that neither death, nor life, nor angels, nor principalities, nor things present, nor things to come, nor powers, nor height, nor depth, nor any other creature, shall be able to separate us from the love of God, which is in Christ Jesus our Lord."

---

[87] Stanza 1 of "Count Your Blessings," composed by Johnson Oatman, 1897.
[88] Romans 8:18, RSV.

For us in America—on this anniversary of September 11th, 2001—the old cliché weighs heavy with truth:

> "I know not what the future holds;
> but I know Who holds the future."[89]

And so, let us conclude today with words from the book of Jude:

> *"Now to him who is able to keep you from falling*
> *and to present you without blemish*
> *before the presence of his glory with rejoicing,*
> *to the only God,*
> *our Savior through Jesus Christ our Lord,*
> *be glory, majesty, dominion, and authority,*
> *before all time and now and for ever. Amen."*[90]

୫ఌ

---

[89] The earliest attribution for this quotation seems to be to the ancient Greek poet Homer (8th or 7th Century, BC). Obviously, the Christian's "Who" is different from his.

[90] Jude 1:24-25, RSV.

115

Romans 10:1-13 ESV

[1] Brothers, my heart's desire and prayer to God for them is that they may be saved. [2] For I bear them witness that they have a zeal for God, but not according to knowledge. [3] For, being ignorant of the righteousness of God, and seeking to establish their own, they did not submit to God's righteousness. [4] For Christ is the end of the law for righteousness to everyone who believes.

[5] For Moses writes about the righteousness that is based on the law, that the person who does the commandments shall live by them. [6] But the righteousness based on faith says, "Do not say in your heart, 'Who will ascend into heaven?'" (that is, to bring Christ down) [7] "or 'Who will descend into the abyss?'" (that is, to bring Christ up from the dead). [8] But what does it say? "The word is near you, in your mouth and in your heart" (that is, the word of faith that we proclaim); [9] because, if you confess with your mouth that Jesus is Lord and believe in your heart that God raised him from the dead, you will be saved. [10] For with the heart one believes and is justified, and with the mouth one confesses and is saved. [11] For the Scripture says, "Everyone who believes in him will not be put to shame." [12] For there is no distinction between Jew and Greek; for the same Lord is Lord of all, bestowing his riches on all who call on him. [13] For "everyone who calls on the name of the Lord will be saved."

⧝

17.

Simple

Romans 10:1-13 ESV

Last week, we went to the store and bought a new computer. We had to; we finally got to the point where we thought we knew how to make the old one work. So, obviously, it was time to get one we didn't understand at all.

When we brought it home, I opened the box, took out the contents, and found a single sheet of paper entitled, "Simple Instructions for Getting Started." I tried to follow the "Simple Instructions," but they turned out to be harder than you would expect. Even with the simple instructions, I had the sense that "getting started" would probably require some expert help.

And so it is with becoming a Christian.

We don't spend much time in our services talking about how to become a Christian. We just sort of assume everybody here is, and go about the business of worship accordingly.

But suppose there is someone here who wants to know how to become a Christian—or someone who thinks that he or she is a Christian, but isn't. Suppose we review the basics this morning—Paul's "simple instructions for getting started"—because, after all, all of us need to be clear about how you become a Christian—about what to tell someone who wants to know.

Now, we're not talking about how to get somebody to *want* to become a Christian: no arm-twisting, no manipulating emotions, no slick religious "sales pitch." No, what do you say when somebody says, "How do I become a Christian?" or shows you in some way that he or she wants to know?

What do you tell your children or your grandchildren, your friend on the fairway or a loved one on a deathbed? What do you say?

"Go see a preacher"?

"Join a church"?

"Read the Bible"?

"Be a good person"?

"Don't worry about it"?

What do you tell them?

How do you become a Christian?

Inquiring minds *might* want to know.

And this question will be on "the final exam," by the way, so you don't want to give the wrong answer. In fact, let me give you a little mental pop quiz right now.

Take out an imaginary piece of paper and an imaginary pencil and write down in your mind how to become a Christian. What do you have to know? What do you have to do?

❧

Okay, time's up—put down your pencils. I'll let you grade your own paper, but before I give you the correct answer, I'll let you know that the natural tendency on this question is to write too much. Most people think there's more to becoming a Christian— or ought to be—than there really is: "To become a Christian, you need to do 'this' and think 'that.'" "You can't be a Christian if you believe 'that' or behave like 'that.'" We become like those politicians who want to stick all those special projects into the legislation that is coming before them.

The correct answer—the "textbook" answer—is laid out very clearly in Romans 10:9: *"If you confess with your lips that 'Jesus is Lord,' and believe in your heart that God has raised him from the dead, you will be saved."*

That's it, folks. And I think it actually will fit in a nutshell.

As a Christian, you should—and do—believe a lot of things. We cover a bunch of them in the creeds we recite together. But the creeds and the theological doctrines we believe are the result of a long, mature reflection on the revelation of scripture, nurtured by sound and continuous Christian education, in the light of the experience of life indwelled by the Holy Spirit.

To *become* a Christian—to begin the journey—you must believe one thing and confess one thing. It sounds simple enough, and it is—remarkably simple: *Believe* and *confess.*

It's simple—but it is not easy. The simple process of becoming a Christian is a very hard one. You don't get to choose the "one thing" you have to believe—or the "one thing" you must confess. And God is the One Who must be satisfied—that you *do* believe what you must believe—and that you *are* confessing what you *must* confess.

⇚⇛

The hardest thing in the world to believe is that God raised Jesus from the dead. The hardest thing in the world to honestly confess is that Jesus is Lord. It's virtually impossible—it *is* humanly impossible—which is why *you* can't do it—you cannot believe what you must believe—you cannot confess what you must confess—without God's help.

And so, when you realize that you do believe that God raised Jesus from the dead, and that you can and will confess that Jesus is Lord, it proves that God is with you and in you, enabling you to do what you could not do by yourself—that is: become a Christian.

And while we're on the subject, notice what Paul says about "believing." To become a Christian, you must believe in your heart

119

that God raised Jesus from the dead—not in your head—but in your heart. Your head is about intellect, logical reasoning, empirical analysis. The heart is the place of conviction and commitment, the haven of hope and faith and love.

You do not have to understand the mechanics of the Resurrection to believe it with your heart. You do not have to have a logical and intellectually compelling answer to the arguments against the Resurrection to decide for yourself that it is a historical reality.

God has given you the ability to believe in your heart what your mind, and other people, will tell you is outside the realm of scientific possibility. To become a Christian, you must exercise that God-given ability to believe with all your heart that the heart of the gospel is true: God raised Jesus from the dead.

The Resurrection of Jesus Christ determines the meaning of everything else in all Creation, including your life and your eternal destiny. That's why it's the one thing you have to believe.

Believe that, and you're halfway there.

વ•ડ

But only halfway.

Believing is half of "how," but it's not all.

The Bible says, in fact, that the demons do that much.[91] The supernatural enemies of God believe—with all their dark and evil hearts—because they know in their minds what we humans can only believe in our hearts on faith. They have not become Christians, however, because they remain firmly rooted in the rebel camp.

To abandon the rebellion against God (and that's your status if you are not a Christian)—to abandon your rebellion against God requires not merely that you recognize that God's side is the right

---

[91] James 2:19.

side, and that you are on the wrong side, and that you should and can change sides.

You must publicly "step over the line"—and announce to God and friend and foe that you have done so. You must declare your allegiance publicly.

You must confess with your lips that *"Jesus is Lord."*

Simple.

You don't have to recite *The Gettysburg Address* or *The Constitution*, or even The Apostles' or Nicene Creed, for that matter. You merely have to confess that *"Jesus is Lord."*

But it's still incredibly hard. And it's hard for several reasons.

One reason is that to confess *"Jesus is Lord"* is also to confess that *you* are not. One of the most attractive features of life as a non-Christian is that you are allowed, even encouraged, to maintain the illusion that you are the lord of your own life—that you call the shots—that you have the right to say what's right and wrong, and how your life will be lived.

You are the center. *You* are the point. It's about *you*—on that side of things. *Your* happiness, *your* satisfaction, *your* success is the ultimate goal if you are not a Christian. *Your* comfort and contentment are the measures of morality.

But even a little bit of life should teach you that this is not the case. If it doesn't, your belief that God has raised Jesus from the dead will.

❧

Another reason that confessing the Lordship of Jesus is hard is this: Even when you believe it—even when you *want* to say it—the world does not want to hear it.

That's why it's called a "confession." Confessing the Lordship of Jesus means telling people where you stand, even when you no longer stand with them.

Confess Jesus as Lord here, in church, and we'll shake your hand. We'll pat you on the back. You might even get a hug or two. We'll be glad that you believe what we believe.

But out in the world, when you tell people you believe that *"Jesus is Lord,"* not only are you saying that *you* are not lord, you are telling them that *they* are not lord, either. You're poking pins in their special balloons. You're pushing them off the comfortable cushions of misguided contentment they're cruising through their lives on. And their natural inclination is to push you back.

☙❧

Do you clam up?

"Oh, *I* don't want to tell anybody I'm a Christian. I'll just keep it to myself. It's a private thing, after all."

Not if you want to become a Christian. Not according to Paul.

You don't have to be pushy or obnoxious, but you do have to notify the world by announcing the truth that has changed your life.

And in doing so, you change the world. Your confession reveals that one more soul has changed sides. You show the world that the God Who did the hardest thing in the world has enabled you to do the hardest thing in your life: to go from death to life— to go from darkness to light—to go from being an enemy of God to being a child and heir of God.

Your confession undermines the illusions people have about their own lordship and confronts them with their need to believe and confess, as you have done—to become a Christian, as you have become.

Do you want to become a Christian?

Believe in your heart that God has raised Jesus from the dead and confess with your lips that *"Jesus is Lord"* and you will be saved. God will make you a Christian.

Believe and confess.

No more and no less.

Simple?

Yes.

Hard?

Incredibly.

But with God's expert help, that's how you do it. That's how you become a Christian.

The most important question on the final exam will be: "Did you?"

...which means the most important question today is "Have you? And if you haven't, will you?"

Will you?

ல்சு

Romans 12:1-2 ESV

¹ I appeal to you therefore, brothers, by the mercies of God, to present your bodies as a living sacrifice, holy and acceptable to God, which is your spiritual worship. ² Do not be conformed to this world, but be transformed by the renewal of your mind, that by testing you may discern what is the will of God, what is good and acceptable and perfect.

❧❦

18.

Different by Design

Romans 12:1-2 ESV

Sometimes, things that seem complicated are really very simple. For instance: How do you live your life as a Christian? It seems very complicated, but it's not. It's simple. You only have two options: conforming to the ways of this world or being transformed for the world to come. The Apostle Paul urges: Go with transformation.

You see, this world is passing away. *You* may not live to see the end of the world. But as a Christian, you will still be around—with God—long after this world is gone. The Resurrection of Jesus Christ means that if you're betting your life on this world, you're betting on a loser.

People do that, of course. They put everything on the familiar, even if it's failed them in the past—even when there's no hope in it for the future. Jesus changed everything, but it's still hard to let go of the old familiar ways, the old dreams and desires this world encourages everyone to chase after.

This world is always pressuring you to get on board—fit in—go along—conform. Whatever the world wants today—that's what you should want. Whatever the current code of conduct is —that's how you should behave.

You want to get along with the world?
Go along.

☙❧

And the truth is that it's not just the world that's always trying to stamp us with its cookie cutter mold. *We* want to fit in as well. We'll go a long way to avoid conflict. And deep down, we still want a lot of what the world is pushing. Conforming is easy. Just let it happen. "Different" draws attention, and for most of us, attention leads to trouble.

Paul knows how the world works. And he knows how the human mind works. And he knows that conforming to this world is the choice most people would like to make—even Christians.

But Paul isn't buying it.

"Do not be conformed to this world." Don't let this world push you down the path of least (or no) resistance.

"Be transformed." Be totally and completely changed. Undergo a metamorphosis. Sounds complicated, but it's not. It's simple.

You can conform yourself to this world. It's a piece of cake. Just let go and let the cultural current carry you along. You can conform yourself.

☙❧

But you cannot *transform* yourself. That takes some serious power—and you don't have it.

On the other hand, you can *be* transformed. You can allow your life and your lifestyle—your attitudes and your actions—to be changed in a fundamental way by the One Who has the power to transform you.

To be transformed from what everybody else in this world is working so hard to be conformed to is certain to make you different—noticeably, aggravatingly different. It's unavoidable—as far as God is concerned.

God wants you different from this world. God wants the world to see the difference. When you accepted all the stuff Paul says in Romans about Jesus—all the stuff about the grace of God in Jesus Christ saving souls—that made your soul different, inside. Now God wants to make your life different on the outside—where people can see it.

And what is your life supposed to look like when God transforms it?

Paul tells the Christians in the Corinthian Church, *"we…are being transformed into the same image"*[92] as what we see in the Lord Jesus.

God wants you to let Him make you look—to this world and the people in it—like another Jesus.

Complicated?

For you, maybe, but not for God, and since God is the One transforming you, it's not really complicated for you, either.

ॐ

So how does God bring about this transformation?

According to Paul, God does it *"through the renewing of your mind."* To take on the likeness of Jesus, you have to take on the mind of Jesus[93] so that you see and understand and value everything as Jesus did, not as the world does. God will radically change your behavior—the way you interact with the world—by completely changing the way you view the world and yourself and God.

Sounds complicated. But again, it's simple, because just as you are not the One doing the transforming of your life, neither are you the One renewing your mind. You are allowing Someone to do it for you. And that Someone is the Holy Spirit.

This isn't the first time this has happened. When Jesus appeared after the Resurrection to the disciples on the Emmaus

---

[92] 2 Corinthians 3:18, ESV.
[93] Philippians 2:5.

Road and later to the disciples in Jerusalem, Luke says *Jesus "opened their minds so they could understand the scriptures."*[94]

In the same way, the Holy Spirit uses the scriptures to renew your mind as the means of transforming your behavior. The reason we emphasize Bible study here at Trinity—and provide you so many opportunities to read and discuss God's Word— is so that the Holy Spirit will have the resources for renewing your mind.

Paul pointed out in 2nd Corinthians, *"...from now on we regard no one from a worldly point of view, though we once regarded Christ in this way...."*[95] The Holy Spirit changed their whole way of thinking by showing them a different way of understanding what the Bible said—first about Jesus, and then about everybody else.

And many of you have started reading the Bible seriously for the first time in your lives. You are delving deeply into the Word of God and coming up with some startling results. Questions, certainly, and lots of them, but you're also experiencing a new spiritual understanding of so many things. You are experiencing the renewing of your minds by the Holy Spirit speaking to you through the scriptures, as the Bible promised. And your lives are being transformed in the process.

&⤸

But that's not the end of it.

You are being transformed by the renewing of your minds— so that you will be able to know from experience the will of God. Because the Holy Spirit is using the Word of God to get you thinking the way Jesus thinks—seeing your life and your world from His perspective—you will come increasingly to recognize the hand of God at work in and around you—just as Jesus did in the events recorded in scripture.

---

[94] Luke 24:32, 45, NIV.
[95] 2 Corinthians 5:17, NIV.

As your mind is renewed, it becomes more and more attuned to God's way of thinking, so that your choices and actions will come more naturally to be what God desires and inspires.

As you do what you have come to see as the will of God, and see the confirmation of God upon your acts of obedience, you will find that you are proving practically that you have an accurate sense of God's will, and will grow in your confidence of your relationship with God.

That's one option for how to live your life as a Christian: Let God transform your life through the Holy Spirit's renewal of your mind, which will result in an enhanced ability to recognize God's will and act effectively in response to it.

This is the preferred option and the one recommended by Paul for all Christians.

ॐ

The other option—the *only* other option—is merely to allow yourself to be conformed to this world. Paul discourages this option. And in the interest of full disclosure, let me unpack the implications of choosing this approach to life.

Because the natural inclination of our sinful human nature is to go along with a sinful society, nothing is required of the individual in this situation except to submit to the culture's continual pressure to conform. No transformational change takes place in the individual because the world wants no such change— and isn't capable of causing it, if it did.

There is no renewing of the mind because there is no serious attention to scripture and no expectation or desire for the Holy Spirit to be involved with the individual in any way. To the extent that there is any change at all, an individual conforming to this world will experience only the accumulation of the world's spiritual weaknesses and the deepening of its moral decay.

The mind that could have been renewed, when conformed to this world, becomes a reprobate mind,[96] according to Paul (in the first chapter of Romans). It does not recognize God's *"good and pleasing and perfect"* will because God abandons this conforming mind to its own worldly and self-destructive obsessions.

These are the two choices. As you can see, choosing really isn't complicated; it's simple.

The contrast is stark and the consequences—well, they have eternal implications.

How do you live your life as a Christian? What will it be?

Conformity or transformation?

This world or the next?

Renewed mind or reprobate?

God's will or God's wrath?

The bad news is that in this monumental decision, one of your options is absolutely awful. The good news is that you're not stuck with the awful option. You have a choice.

Two options. One choice.

Choose divine transformation and all that goes with it.

It's just that simple.

૭✦৭

---

[96] Romans 1:28, KJV.

19.

Love, Hate and Hold on Tight

Romans 12:9-21 NRSV

⁹ Let love be genuine; hate what is evil, hold fast to what is good; ¹⁰ love one another with mutual affection; outdo one another in showing honor. ¹¹ Do not lag in zeal, be ardent in spirit, serve the Lord. ¹² Rejoice in hope, be patient in suffering, persevere in prayer. ¹³ Contribute to the needs of the saints; extend hospitality to strangers.

¹⁴ Bless those who persecute you; bless and do not curse them. ¹⁵ Rejoice with those who rejoice, weep with those who weep. ¹⁶ Live in harmony with one another; do not be haughty, but associate with the lowly; do not claim to be wiser than you are. ¹⁷ Do not repay anyone evil for evil, but take thought for what is noble in the sight of all. ¹⁸ If it is possible, so far as it depends on you, live peaceably with all. ¹⁹ Beloved, never avenge yourselves, but leave room for the wrath of God; for it is written, "Vengeance is mine, I will repay, says the Lord." ²⁰ No, "if your enemies are hungry, feed them; if they are thirsty, give them something to drink; for by doing this you will heap burning coals on their heads." ²¹ Do not be overcome by evil, but overcome evil with good.

❧⊰

In today's reading from Romans, you heard a whole laundry list of spiritual and moral "do's and don'ts" that Paul laid on the Christians in Rome.

These are spiritual rules, which means: Not only are they not normal for us, they are not even possible for us—without the help of the Holy Spirit.

But since the Holy Spirit dwells within us, they are attitudes and actions that are now possible. They are also necessary and required for citizens of the kingdom of God, even if they are not yet automatic.

Look at the first three: Let love be genuine. Hate what is evil. Hold fast to what is good.

Paul says, *"Let love be genuine."* That which is "genuine" is not fake, insincere or hypocritical. "Genuine" is the opposite of counterfeit. Genuine love will cost you more than fake love, just as genuine art will cost you more than the cheap imitations.

Paul directs us to invest ourselves in genuine love, to settle for nothing less in our lives and in our fellowship than the true masterpiece of godly love, framed in compassion and displayed in sacrificial service.

Jesus put it another way: *"Love your neighbor as yourself."* [97] The love we feel for ourselves is genuine. It's the real thing. We're not faking it. We really do love ourselves. You and I will do just about anything to make ourselves happy, to ease our own pain, to protect ourselves from danger.

"Okay," says Jesus (echoed by Paul), "love others the same way." Take the same perspective—invest the same energy and resources—make the same sacrifices—for others. Love everybody that same way: genuinely.

☙❧

But Christianity is not all love. Love others genuinely, but hate evil passionately. The word translated "hate" means to detest—to recoil from something with revulsion. Evil should turn your stomach; it ought to make you sick.

---

[97] Matthew 22:39, RSV.

You should hate evil so much that you can't stand the sight or the sound of it—the touch or the taste or the smell of it.

Oh, we can hate evil in others, often vigorously and gleefully. We hate more evil in others sometimes than is actually there. We can find the evil speck in someone else's eye with a telescope,[98] but it's harder to find one with a mirror: "Oh, well, that's just a personality quirk of mine. I don't mean anything by it."

But it is evil. There is evil in us. And it is doing what evil does—in us—physically, spiritually, morally and socially.

Don't let anyone tell you, "It's not so bad once you get used to it." Evil *is* so bad, even when you get used to it—*especially* when you get used to it—because then you don't fight it—you don't resist it. You let it loose in you to do what it does.

The corruption, destruction and death in evil don't change just because it is at work in you. If you endure what you should abhor, you will come to accept it and eventually embrace it.

See evil for what it is, and hate it for what it is, and use the power of that passion to drive it out and keep it out. Hate what is evil.

❧

But when it comes to the good: Hold on for dear life. Good—in this world, anyway—is not a "gimme." It's not automatic, any more than genuine love is. Don't assume that you can neglect the good for a while and it will be there when you come back. Don't assume that it will follow you like a shadow on a sunny day. Good has enemies in this world—evil is out to corrupt or nullify or destroy every aspect of good it can.[99]

And…good as you may be (or think you are), goodness is not a natural trait for any of us. It is a gift from God that must be cherished and nurtured and embraced with determination.

---

98 Matthew 7:3.
99 Luke 8:12; Acts 13:10.

"Hold it fast," says Paul, using the same word Luke used in Acts, Chapter 8, to describe Philip's grip on the Ethiopian ambassador's chariot as it raced through the desert.[100]

Jesus used the same word to describe a prodigal son attaching himself like glue to an indifferent farmer to keep from starving to death.[101]

Hold on to anything and everything good like your life depends on it. If you don't, the good will slip through your fingers, or fade away while your back is turned. Don't let go of the good—no matter what!

As Christians, love genuinely, hate evil, hold on tight to the good. There's more to being a Christian, of course.

But these will do for a start.

கூ⊸ே

---

[100] Acts 8:29.
[101] Luke 11:14-15.

20.

Understanding the Time

Romans 13:11-14 ESV

¹¹ ...you know the time, that the hour has come for you to wake from sleep. For salvation is nearer to us now than when we first believed. ¹² The night is far gone; the day is at hand. So then let us cast off the works of darkness and put on the armor of light. ¹³ Let us walk properly as in the daytime, not in orgies and drunkenness, not in sexual immorality and sensuality, not in quarreling and jealousy. ¹⁴ But put on the Lord Jesus Christ, and make no provision for the flesh, to gratify its desires.

❧

I would like to begin the sermon with a little experiment today. Would you help me? Those of you listening on the radio are welcome to participate at home. If you're listening in the car, just drive; this could get complicated.

First of all, will those of you who are left-handed, please raise your right hand? It's all right; you're not voting for anything or enlisting in the service. Leave your hands up for a moment. Now, will the right-handers please raise your left hand? Good.

Now, notice how many of these uplifted arms have wristwatches attached to them.

We are a people determined to know what time it is, at any second, down to the second. We wear these watches so we can check the time, anytime. If you take a quick look, you will all know the time, right now. Thank you, you can put your hands—and your watches—down.

I know it's probably not wise for a preacher to call your attention to the time at the beginning of a sermon. I hope you won't feel the need to look at your watches again—at least until I'm finished. If you do, I'll have nobody to blame but myself, I'm sure.

കൗൻ

What was the purpose of this little exercise?

The purpose was to make a point—and a distinction.

The point is that we are a group of Christians who know the time—with pinpoint accuracy.

And the distinction?

That the kind of time we've been talking about is not the kind of time Paul is talking about in the passage from Romans we read earlier.

Paul wrote to the Christians in Rome almost two thousand years ago. They had no Rolexes or Timexes or Seikos. With their sundials and hourglasses, they were lucky if they could tell the difference between "quarter after" and "ten till."

Furthermore, there were no time zones—no Daylight-Saving Time—no standardization of time measurement from one country to the next—or even one village to the next. Paul's letter to the Roman Christians would have taken weeks—perhaps months—to get from him to them. He would have no way of knowing what time it would be when they received it or read it out to the group.

But Paul assumed they "knew the time." He didn't know them; he'd never been to Rome. But they were Christians and so he could write to them with confidence that they "knew the time." Paul assumed that to be a Christian means you know something about time that those who have not believed in Jesus don't know.

So, do you "know the time"? Do you? Or are you finding yourself a little hazy on the subject just now?

I mentioned a moment ago a distinction: Paul is talking about time, but it is a different kind of time. He is even using a different word. The word for "tick-tick-tick" time—the time on your watch (don't look, just trust me on this)—that word is χρόνος—*"chronos."* That's why Navy clocks are called "chronometers" and a listing of things in the time sequence they happened in is called a "chronology."

But there is another kind of time—a special, "not-like-time" time—a time when time stands still or has nothing to do with the passage of that *chronos* time. We sense it when babies are born or wedding vows are spoken. There's a sense of it in the worst moments of war and the holiest moments of worship. There is another time—sometimes intersecting the mundane, everyday *chronos* time—sometimes arching far above and beyond it. It is God's time.

Paul calls it καιρός—*"kairos."* And it is everything that *chronos* is not. *Chronos* time moves with the certainty of the tides and waits for no man. *Kairos* time, on the other hand, has the patience of God and is so tied to eternity that God has all the time—not merely "in the world"—but in all the worlds in all Creation, and in the infinity of space between and around and beyond all those worlds.

Chronos time is the time it takes for animal, vegetable or mineral to get from Point A to Point B. *Chronos* time is measurable; *kairos* time is not—it's miraculous. *Kairos* time is the time it takes for God to restore His fallen Creation and to draw your sinful heart to Him. *Kairos* is the time it takes for a Messiah to be born in a manger and to die on a Cross and to rise from the dead. It's a different kind of time: It's God's time.

Of course, *kairos* time is so different from *chronos* time that a lot of people don't realize that such a thing exists. You can tell them there's a time unlike our time and, a lot of times, they just won't believe it. They don't know the time—the *kairos* time.

കൃ

But you do—if you're a Christian.

The time you became a Christian was *kairos* time. You may remember the hour and day, the place and the circumstances, the *chronos* details. But the moment when you meet Jesus is a *kairos* moment—always. It only happens in God's time.

The time you spend with Jesus is *kairos* time, even if you measure it off in the minutes and hours of *chronos*. God's time and our time intersect, but they are never the same.

They are so different, in fact, that it's like the difference between being awake and being asleep. You can cruise through your life on autopilot, oblivious to some or all of what's going on around you or within you. You can devote your life to a detailed schedule or leave it to chance or fate to fill in the hours of your day. But if you're not paying attention to that other kind of time— that *kairos* time—you're not really cruizin'; you're snoozin'.

That's why Paul says, *"You know the time."* You've met Jesus. You've experienced the Holy Spirit coming into you. You've stepped into *kairos* time for a moment. Don't forget it—or ignore it—or let it pass you by. You know there is a *kairos* time—God's time. Don't get distracted by *chronos* time and everything that happens there. *Chronos* is just our way of going from Point A to B to C. Wake up to what God is doing in His special, eternal time.

Once you have met Jesus, you can live in both times, not just one. But to do this, to spend *kairos* time with Jesus, not just *chronos* time studying or thinking about Him—going through the motions—you must go beyond *knowing* the time to *understanding* the time—understanding that there is a reality where you spend your life in the presence of God and in loving relationship with Him. To live your life with the holy One Who has given you life, you have to wake up from your *chronos* life to the *kairos* life.

Sometimes, when I'm all warm and comfortable and not really paying attention to things, I've been known to nod off. One minute I'm awake and the next I'm asleep and I don't even realize it until I start to slip and I startle myself back to consciousness. Some of you may be having that same experience right now.

Paul says, "Wake up! You know about *kairos* time. You understand what it is. You've been there with Jesus. It's not just something that happened 'way back when,' one day in *chronos* time."

It's God time all the time: when God saved you, and every time God speaks to you and blesses you and reaches out to touch your life. It's your special time with God now. And God wants it to be all the time, and it can be, if you don't slip back into the other time where nobody thinks about God's time or even knows it exists.

Chronos and *kairos* are as different as night and day. But Paul says the night is just about over; the day is about to dawn.

So, get up, you spiritual sleepy head! "Rise and shine and give God the glory!"[102] Throw off the dark deeds of your *chronos* time like a blanket that's in the way and jump into God's *kairos* reality like a new set of clothes.

If you get focused on this world—this time—all you'll do is *chronos* stuff. Punch the clock. Work your job. Get ahead if you can. Have a little fun. Hang on till you die.

But if you understand the *kairos*—the reality of God's time and its fullness revealed in Jesus Christ—you can put on, not just the armor of light God has given you for this time, but the very essence of the Lord Himself.

Kairos and *chronos* are worlds apart—as far apart as this world is from the next.

Or at least you would think they were, if you didn't know and understand about *kairos* time. If you know anything about *kairos*—

---

[102] "Rise, Shine, and Give God the Glory," a traditional Christian children's song.

understand anything about this miraculous time when the reality of God and His eternity entangles itself in love and grace with the plodding predictability of our time—you know that it's so close *all* the time that you can reach out and touch it—or rather that God can (and does) reach out of it and touch you and take your hand and lead you into His sacred and supernatural time, if you will let Him.

ॐ

How do you tell people about *kairos* when they only know *chronos*—only understand *chronos*—only believe *chronos*?

You tell them about things that happened when God placed a *kairos* moment alongside a *chronos* one. Three of our members did that on Wednesday night when they testified to God's generosity in their lives—and the gratitude they were able to reach across time and give Him. The Anderson family added a *kairos* moment to our *chronos* time this morning as they lit a Candle of Hope[103] in our seemingly hopeless world.

And we will all point to the *kairos* time of God over the next few weeks when we repeat the story we have settled securely into our chronological calendars: the story of a *kairos* moment when a virgin gave birth to a Baby and angels sang and shepherds wondered and wise men came and worshipped.

Old story—new truth.

On a day like any other and yet like no other, two times came together—*chronos* and *kairos*—and the heaven of God touched the world of mankind.

Tell them that, if they do not understand the time. Tell them God's salvation is even closer to us—now—than when we first believed. And it can be just as close to them.

---

[103] The Candle of Hope on an Advent Wreath is lit on the First Sunday in Advent.

Well, time's up—for the sermon, I mean. It has a chronological limit.

But the *message* of this sermon is a part of God's *kairos* time. The message will keep on going—in the timeless time of God—if you tell it.

ॐ

Romans 14:1-12 NRSV

¹ *Welcome those who are weak in faith, but not for the purpose of quarreling over opinions.* ² *Some believe in eating anything, while the weak eat only vegetables.* ³ *Those who eat must not despise those who abstain, and those who abstain must not pass judgment on those who eat; for God has welcomed them.* ⁴ *Who are you to pass judgment on servants of another? It is before their own lord that they stand or fall. And they will be upheld, for the Lord is able to make them stand.*

⁵ *Some judge one day to be better than another, while others judge all days to be alike. Let all be fully convinced in their own minds.* ⁶ *Those who observe the day, observe it in honor of the Lord. Also those who eat, eat in honor of the Lord, since they give thanks to God; while those who abstain, abstain in honor of the Lord and give thanks to God.*

⁷ *We do not live to ourselves, and we do not die to ourselves.* ⁸ *If we live, we live to the Lord, and if we die, we die to the Lord; so then, whether we live or whether we die, we are the Lord's.* ⁹ *For to this end Christ died and lived again, so that he might be Lord of both the dead and the living.*

¹⁰ *Why do you pass judgment on your brother or sister? Or you, why do you despise your brother or sister? For we will all stand before the judgment seat of God.* ¹¹ *For it is written,*

> *"As I live, says the Lord,*
> *every knee shall bow to me,*
> *and every tongue shall give praise to God."*

¹² *So then, each of us will be accountable to God.*

৵•৻

21.

Getting Along, Weak and Strong

Romans 14:1-12 NRSV

One of my favorite hymns is "The Church's One Foundation."[104] The foundation they're referring to is "Jesus Christ her Lord." You would think with the "one Lord, one faith, one birth" the hymn celebrates, the Church would be unified the way Jesus wants it to be.

But it's not. We're human and we see things differently, even as Christians—even as the Church. And we often act accordingly, messing up the fellowship and undermining our witness to the world in the bargain. This is not good.

Nor is it new.

Paul was talking about it in Romans 14 and 15, and it was not one of those "just in case" conversations. Christians were choosing sides in the Church, consciously or unconsciously. Any time this happens in the Church, it's a problem. It happened then, and it happens today.

In Paul's case, the issue was the proper lifestyle for Christians, and the issue was splitting the Roman Church (and others). Paul called the two factions: "the weak" and "the strong."

---

[104] Samuel John Stone, "The Church's One Foundation," 1866.

The "weak" Christians were those who severely limited their diets for religious reasons and honored traditional holidays and rituals.

The "strong" were those who latched onto Paul's concept of "religious liberty" and ran with it.

స్తుతి

Notice that the "weak" Christians were the people exercising self-discipline and self-sacrifice. They showed more commitment to Christianity in their behavior than the "strong" Christians did.

The "weak" folks were considered weak because they couldn't seem to grasp that Jesus set people free from the old bondage to religious rules and regulations.

The "strong" folks were those whose faith was strong enough to believe that salvation really was a free gift and not earned or maintained by good deeds.

The weak Christians were sure the others were going to hell because they wouldn't get with the "right beliefs and behavior" program: "You can't really be a Christian if you think and act *that* way!"

The strong Christians just found the weak people dense. To them, the weak Christians had no imagination—no appreciation for the radical new nature of life in Christ. The strong Christians knew they were set free from sin and restored to right relationship with God by grace, apart from the requirements of the Law. They thought: "These religious fanatics among us are so tedious!"

స్తుతి

And Paul told both sides to knock it off.

The "weak" Christians (Today, we call them "conservatives.") are to stop consigning the "strong" Christians (now called "liberals") to hell—or intermediate points along the way.

The liberals in the Church—Paul's "strong" faction—are to stop looking down their obviously superior noses at these people they view and value as something less than clueless sheep.

Isn't it interesting that when Paul wrote to the Romans, the conservatives were the vegetarians and the liberals were the red-meat lovers? Some of the issues have changed over the centuries; the attitudes and tendencies that hinder the unity of the fellowship have not.

Now we divide up sides over what clothes people should wear to church and what music to sing and how loud. Our three distinct worship services are ready-made for factionalism unless we guard ourselves and our thinking, remembering that we are all one congregation—one chapel family—one church body.

This is not to say that there are no rights and wrongs in the Church. The gospel of Jesus Christ is certainly not "anything goes." It's the gospel of the world that takes that approach.

Our God is a righteous God. There is that which pleases Him and that which He opposes. But until we are all in perfect accord and all know for sure about everything in God's agenda, we are all to see our different perspectives about the things of God and this world as honest efforts to see and do God's will.

༜

And one more thing.

Paul's admonition applies to politics as well. An important election looms before us. We Christians have become passionate about our politics. We are often so certain we know God's mind on an issue that we cannot conceive how any "genuine" Christian could possibly see it any other way.

And yet, professing Christians fall out all over the political spectrum. We are not to judge anyone's Christianity based on his or her politics. Nor are we to become un-Christian in our treatment of people—and especially other professing Christians—who hold political positions we strongly oppose. Argue the issues, but do not undermine the unity of the Church in the process.

Whatever the outcome of the election, we will still be the Church. And our Lord will still be our Lord. And He will expect and demand that we live together in unity, on the sure foundation He has provided.

৯৵৽

Romans 14:3-11 ESV

³ Let not the one who eats despise the one who abstains, and let not the one who abstains pass judgment on the one who eats, for God has welcomed him. ⁴ Who are you to pass judgment on the servant of another? It is before his own master that he stands or falls. And he will be upheld, for the Lord is able to make him stand.

⁵ One person esteems one day as better than another, while another esteems all days alike. Each one should be fully convinced in his own mind. ⁶ The one who observes the day, observes it in honor of the Lord. The one who eats, eats in honor of the Lord, since he gives thanks to God, while the one who abstains, abstains in honor of the Lord and gives thanks to God. ⁷ For none of us lives to himself, and none of us dies to himself. ⁸ For if we live, we live to the Lord, and if we die, we die to the Lord. So then, whether we live or whether we die, we are the Lord's. ⁹ For to this end Christ died and lived again, that he might be Lord both of the dead and of the living.

¹⁰ Why do you pass judgment on your brother? Or you, why do you despise your brother? For we will all stand before the judgment seat of God; ¹¹ for it is written,

> *"As I live, says the Lord,*
> *every knee shall bow to me,*
> *and every tongue shall confess to God."*

Matthew 18:21-35 ESV

[21] *Then Peter came up and said to [Jesus], "Lord, how often will my brother sin against me, and I forgive him? As many as seven times?"* [22] *Jesus said to him, "I do not say to you seven times, but seventy-seven times.*

[23] *"Therefore the kingdom of heaven may be compared to a king who wished to settle accounts with his servants.* [24] *When he began to settle, one was brought to him who owed him ten thousand talents.* [25] *And since he could not pay, his master ordered him to be sold, with his wife and children and all that he had, and payment to be made.* [26] *So the servant fell on his knees, imploring him, 'Have patience with me, and I will pay you everything.'* [27] *And out of pity for him, the master of that servant released him and forgave him the debt.* [28] *But when that same servant went out, he found one of his fellow servants who owed him a hundred denarii, and seizing him, he began to choke him, saying, 'Pay what you owe.'* [29] *So his fellow servant fell down and pleaded with him, 'Have patience with me, and I will pay you.'* [30] *He refused and went and put him in prison until he should pay the debt.* [31] *When his fellow servants saw what had taken place, they were greatly distressed, and they went and reported to their master all that had taken place.* [32] *Then his master summoned him and said to him, 'You wicked servant! I forgave you all that debt because you pleaded with me.* [33] *And should not you have had mercy on your fellow servant, as I had mercy on you?'* [34] *And in anger his master delivered him to the jailers, until he should pay all his debt.* [35] *So also my heavenly Father will do to every one of you, if you do not forgive your brother from your heart."*

જ⚬ઉ

22.

Unity, Liberty, Charity

Romans 14:3-11; Matthew 18:21-35 ESV

We are an interdenominational church. It says so, right on our logo—right under our name. It's in small letters—you'll probably need a magnifying glass to see it on the back of your bulletin—but it's there: "Trinity Christian Fellowship—An Interdenominational Church."

And we put that "identifier" there right at the very beginning—right from the start.

Right from the start, we decided to be different—we decided to be a fellowship of Christians who agree to disagree.

And we do disagree—about a lot of things. You have to, if some are going to be Baptists, and some Catholics, and others Methodists and Lutherans and Presbyterians and Episcopalians and whatever else, and some nothing at all because they—*you*—have never had a label or you've tried most all of them at one time or another.

People who don't know us have asked me, "What's Trinity's position on this issue?" or "What does your church believe about 'that'?"

Well, first of all, it's not *my* church.

But more importantly, I have to tell them, "We've probably got a lot of positions on that issue," and "I'd have to ask around to see what all we believe about that particular doctrine or interpretation."

Each denomination has nailed down its unique beliefs for its adherents—in many cases, a long time ago. But we're a little bit of all of them—we have some of all of these denominations represented in our fellowship—so we're something of a patchwork quilt theologically.

"But how can you do that? How could that possibly work?"

The only way it can work is the way Paul told the Christians in the church in Rome to make it work. He said, "Do everything to be unified and nothing to be uniform."

When you join a church—or start one—the natural tendency is to expect that you will agree with the rest of the people—and they, with you. And when you discover you don't agree with somebody about something—and sooner or later you *will* discover that—it can really bother you. The natural tendency is to try to get everybody to agree—which usually means trying to get "them" to agree with "us"—since, after all, "we" are obviously right.

Now, we do agree about a lot of things. I think we agree about the important things; we are unified by our shared commitment to the essence of Christianity, otherwise, we could not cope with not agreeing about so many other things. But disagreeing is still uncomfortable—and has its risks.

❧❦

The church in Rome had disagreements. And their disagreements were causing factions—threatening their spiritual unity. And even though it wasn't Paul's church—he had not founded it or even visited it—he was willing to talk to them about how to deal with their differences. And he did it in an interesting way.

Paul labeled the factions. But he did not call them "right" or "wrong." He called them the "weak" and the "strong." And here's where it gets interesting.

Contrary to what you might expect, he called the more devout ones—the ones who sacrificed more and worked harder to practice their faith—the "weak" ones.

Those who didn't do a lot to distinguish themselves from the rest of the world, Paul labeled the "strong"—and appears to have placed himself squarely in their camp.

"But that can't be right! Surely, the people who put more effort into being Christians are better Christians. Surely, they're the 'strong' Christians."

Not according to Paul.

The way Paul sees it, being a Christian is not, first of all, about what *you* do, but about how "strongly" you believe that Jesus Christ has done all that needs to be done for you to be right with God and free from the condemnation of sin. The "strong" are those who are able to believe that Jesus made everything okay.

The "weak" are those who "believe," but feel the need to hedge their bets just a bit by submitting themselves to special diets and paying special attention to special days on the calendar, just in case God cares about those things.

Now, Paul may also have called the "strong" the "strong" because there were more of them in the church than the others. It appears that they were in the majority, because most of what Paul says about preserving the unity of the church, he says to them.

❧

Paul says, "Accept the weaker folks into the church—welcome them—and not just so that you can harass them for being different from you. Respect them—and the things that make them different from you."

But preserving the unity of the Church is not just the responsibility of some of the members.

It's everybody's job—however you go about "doing" your Christianity.

To the more devout and self-sacrificing believers, Paul says, "No judging the easy-going guys as deficient in faith or spiritual maturity. They belong to God and God will judge them—just as you belong to God and God will judge you."

And here's some good news for "strong" and "weak" alike, if you're willing to hear it: God accepts you both.

God accepts you both, not because you're right in how you've decided to practice your faith, but because, however you're practicing it, you're doing what you believe will please God—you want to please God. And when you share that desire—that commitment—you are unified in Christ—the "strong" with the "weak"—whatever your differences.

"But do you know how aggravating it is to show up for a pot luck supper at church and see these guys turn their noses up at our food because it's not good enough—not pure enough—for them? And every time we turn around, we're looked down on because we shouldn't be out having some good clean fun on some day they decided was holy."

"Yea? Well, we're trying to live dedicated Christian lives in this moral cesspool of a city—to be good witnesses for the gospel—and people in our own church act like we are lunatics and live like the ways of the world around us are really just fine."

And Paul says, "Yes. You're different. Now, get along! Both sides are saved. Both sides are acceptable to God. Both of you are doing what you're doing as your best effort to honor God. Respect and accept each other as the servants of God you all are—for the unity of the Body that is more important to God than what any of you is doing."

అ~అ

"But how?"

Maybe what Jesus told Peter applies here: Practice repeated forgiveness.[105]

Every time you're exasperated, give your aggravation to God and your forgiveness and forbearance to your Christian brother or sister. Ask yourself, "What is God doing in these folks whose behavior bothers me so much?" And then, ask yourself, "What is God doing in me as I deal with these folks whose behavior bothers me so much?"

In Rome, they were getting worked up over things like whether meat should be on the Christian menu and when and how to hold a religious holiday. For Christians today, we can divide up sides over equaling pressing matters like what to wear to church and what kind of music to sing when we get here and where should we put the words for you to sing (or not sing) by.

Churches break up over what version of the Bible to read and what color the carpets should be. Sooner or later, we're actually going to get to decide where to build our church and how to pay for it.

Whatever side you chose on any of these or other issues, no doubt you will have a reason that is compelling for you. The same will be true for those who disagree with you. And none of that releases you, or any of us, from our obligation to God to preserve the unity of our fellowship.

Fortunately, right or wrong—weak or strong—because we are committed to the unity of the Body—we are all growing deeper in faith and closer to Christ. Though there are differences in the way we practice our faith, we allow room for each other to grow, and we encourage one another in the un-uniform process, so that we all move forward—often out of step—but always advancing together to the glorious goal God has set for us all in Christ Jesus.

That's why we like to quote one of the leaders of the Protestant Reformation to describe our fellowship:

[105] Matthew 18:21-22.

"In Essentials: Unity;
In Non-essentials: Liberty;
In All Things: Charity."[106]

১৯৯৩

Unity—liberty—charity—Trinity. There is something to be said for an interdenominational church—if it's a fellowship where the "weak" and the "strong" will live lovingly with one another.

১৯৯৩

---

[106] Attributed to Philip Melanchthon (1497-1560).

From the 1st Letter to the Corinthians

1 Corinthians 2:1-12 ESV

[1] And I, when I came to you, brothers, did not come proclaiming to you the testimony of God with lofty speech or wisdom. [2] For I decided to know nothing among you except Jesus Christ and him crucified. [3] And I was with you in weakness and in fear and much trembling, [4] and my speech and my message were not in plausible words of wisdom, but in demonstration of the Spirit and of power, [5] so that your faith might not rest in the wisdom of men but in the power of God.

[6] Yet among the mature we do impart wisdom, although it is not a wisdom of this age or of the rulers of this age, who are doomed to pass away. [7] But we impart a secret and hidden wisdom of God, which God decreed before the ages for our glory. [8] None of the rulers of this age understood this, for if they had, they would not have crucified the Lord of glory. [9] But, as it is written,

> *"What no eye has seen, nor ear heard,*
> *nor the heart of man imagined,*
> *what God has prepared*
> *for those who love him"—*

[10] these things God has revealed to us through the Spirit. For the Spirit searches everything, even the depths of God. [11] For who knows a person's thoughts except the spirit of that person, which is in him? So also no one comprehends the thoughts of God except the Spirit of God. [12] Now we have received not the spirit of the world, but the Spirit who is from God, that we might understand the things freely given us by God.

৵৹৻

23.

A Different Kind of Wisdom

1 Corinthians 2:1-12 ESV

"You are *SO* stupid!"

That's what they think, you know. Anyone in this modern world who still hangs on to the "nonsense" about Jesus Christ—this nonsense about there being some kind of salvation through His Crucifixion and Resurrection—is considered laughable—unworthy of respect or serious consideration—certainly gullible, and probably dangerous, if allowed to do anything based on those beliefs.

I first encountered that secular snobbery in high school from a few classmates who had jumped on the cultural bandwagon of "the 60s." Now our children get it in grammar school, and not just from the other children. Tolerance and respect for the beliefs of others? Absolutely—unless they involve faith in the crucified Christ.

It used to be that they just *thought* you were stupid. Now, they're willing—even eager—to *tell* you what they think: "How can you believe that stuff? It's stupid! And so are you, if you believe it!"

What's this modern world coming to?

The same thing the ancient world came to—at least as far as Christianity is concerned.

The first Christians faced the same hostility to their faith in Jesus we do. To the smart people of their day, the idea of worshipping Someone Who had been tortured and executed was ridiculous. To believe there was any benefit to be gained by accepting what Christians like Paul were saying about Jesus was thought insane.

And Paul didn't clean the story up any, either. He didn't soft-pedal the parts they were laughing at. He didn't try to dazzle anybody with sophisticated philosophical footwork. Just Jesus Christ. Crucified.

So why—if that's so stupid—are we here? Why is the Chapel here, and all the other churches and congregations of Christian "idiots"? Why has Christianity survived the ridicule and the disdain of all the smart people in the world for centuries? Why didn't the gullible saps who got snookered into Christianity in the beginning come to their senses when the more intelligent folks clued them in to their stupidity? Why are people still believing the gospel of Jesus Christ when they hear it today, when all the smart people know better?

The gospel of Jesus Christ—the idea that His being crucified does anything of any value for anybody—is—from a human point of view—absolutely illogical—beyond reason.

శ్రీ-్ళ

But suppose there is another point of view—a divine point of view.

Suppose there *is* a God, and that the attitude and actions of this God are so infinitely superior to human experience that what this God says and does simply defies the logic of the greatest human minds. That's at least conceivable.

But then suppose that the attitudes and actions of this infinitely superior and humanly indiscernible God are, nonetheless, accurately represented in the events that Christians proclaim as their gospel. Could a God Who cannot be discovered by any human wisdom choose to reveal Himself to us in a way that makes human wisdom useless—or worse? And if God could and did commit a little "revelation," who's going to know, and how?

Well, a lot of stupid people like you and me have ignored the wisdom of the world long enough to accept the good news that a Christ had come from God and been crucified—as God had planned—for us.

And what did we find out when we accepted that gospel?

We came in contact with another wisdom—a deeper wisdom—a wisdom that looks stupid from the outside—but turns out to be brilliant on the inside.

It's like going into a dark cave and discovering a priceless treasure hidden inside. You can't see any treasure looking into the cave from the outside. And that's not where anybody would have hidden a treasure—or so you might think.

So, for those reasons, a lot of people will not go into the cave to look. Those of us who say, "There is a treasure in there," are doubted by those who are convinced they know better.

But people who find the treasure are just not going to be convinced there is no treasure—not by those who won't even look in the cave. And people who find a priceless treasure are rich, no matter how clever and sophisticated the people are who try to tell them they aren't.

In fact, those who are telling the people with the treasure how stupid they are seem themselves a little stupid for refusing to go and get some of the treasure for themselves. Just because you don't think there should be a treasure where people are finding it doesn't mean it isn't there.

It just means you won't accept a reality you didn't think up yourself. It means while they get rich, you stay poor, no matter how smart you think you are.

I saw a bumper sticker one time that read, "If you're so smart, why ain't you rich?" The next time you hear some wise guy waxing eloquent about the intellectual inferiority of your faith in the crucified Christ, you might want to ask him that question—as you enjoy the treasure God has given you.

ॐ⊷ॐ

24.

Your Body—His Temple

1 Corinthians 6:12-20 NRSV

[12] "All things are lawful for me," but not all things are beneficial. "All things are lawful for me," but I will not be dominated by anything. [13] "Food is meant for the stomach and the stomach for food," and God will destroy both one and the other. The body is meant not for fornication but for the Lord, and the Lord for the body. [14] And God raised the Lord and will also raise us by his power. [15] Do you not know that your bodies are members of Christ? Should I therefore take the members of Christ and make them members of a prostitute? Never! [16] Do you not know that whoever is united to a prostitute becomes one body with her? For it is said, "The two shall be one flesh." [17] But anyone united to the Lord becomes one spirit with him. [18] Shun fornication! Every sin that a person commits is outside the body; but the fornicator sins against the body itself. [19] Or do you not know that your body is a temple of the Holy Spirit within you, which you have from God, and that you are not your own? [20] For you were bought with a price; therefore glorify God in your body.

❧❦

In the Old Testament, a king named Josiah is praised for repairing a Jerusalem Temple that had been neglected and misused, and in the New Testament Gospels, Jesus cleanses the Jerusalem

Temple of His day and reclaims it for the worship of God by driving people out of it who are perverting its sacred purpose.[107]

You and I are here in Chapel Hall again this morning because we are cleaning up the Chapel sanctuary, our "temple," the place where we normally go to meet our God.

In each case, there is a deep and determined commitment to put the house of God, the physical place set aside for Him, in the proper condition to honor Him and encounter His holy Presence.

But not all temples are made with human hands.[108] Not all of the physical sanctuaries designed for the dwelling of Almighty God are buildings with steeples, pulpits and pews.

The apostle Paul says, *"...your body is a temple of the Holy Spirit."* Where does he come up with that?

Well, Jesus told His disciples the night before He was crucified, *"...I will pray the Father, and he will give you another Counselor to be with you forever...the Spirit of truth...you know him, for he dwells with you, and will be in you."*[109]

And so Paul can say a few chapters earlier in 1st Corinthians, *"Don't you know that you are God's temple and that God's Spirit dwells in you? ...God's temple is holy, and you are that temple."*[110]

When Paul says, *"Don't you know..."* he's really saying, "I know you know, but you're sure not acting like it." Every Christian is now a temple of God. Every Christian's body, according to Paul, is now a permanent, physical location of the Holy Spirit.

❧

Notice that Paul says, "body"—not mind, spirit, or soul.

Your body is the dwelling place of God Himself in all His holiness, glory and power. That familiar form you were looking at in the mirror this morning is a temple of the Holy Spirit of God.

---

[107] 2 Kings 23:1-14, 25; John 2:13-17.
[108] Acts 7:48; 2 Corinthians 5:1; Hebrews 9:24.
[109] John 14:16-17, RSV.
[110] 1 Corinthians 3:16-18, NRSV.

Yes, that's another good reason for losing weight and getting in shape, but Paul's going after another matter. Paul is saying, "I know you know, that with the Holy Spirit dwelling permanently in your physical body, your body is a temple—a sanctuary, every bit as much as any sacred building erected to worship God. But you're not acting like you know it in what you are doing with your body."

Now, what the Corinthian Christians were doing with their temple bodies was pretty much what our modern society is doing: having sex with whomever they can, whenever they can, under whatever circumstances exist. Our modern sexual revolution is not modern at all, of course; it is merely a throwing off of the moral protection we had provided ourselves as a result of countless generations of painful experience that proved God's warning that sex outside His purpose will always do harm to those involved—and others.

So knock off the prostitution, and the pre-marital and extra-marital sex (and let's throw in internet and cable pornography, for modern day good measure) because what you're doing with your body with the Holy Spirit in it, you're making the Holy Spirit do *with* you, because the Holy Spirit is in your physical body.

☙◊❧

Not presently engaged in any ungodly sexual activity?

Good. Then let's expand our application of the principle.

Whatever you are doing with or to your body, you are doing it with and to the Holy Spirit in you.

Are you abusing your body in any way?

Then you are abusing the Holy Spirit Who dwells in that body.

Are you devoting yourself to physical activities that are unworthy of or contrary to the will of God?

You are not just being sinful yourself; you are taking the Holy Spirit along for the ride.

Okay, enough guilt-tripping. Let's finish up focused on the flip side.

If you know that your body is the temple of the Holy Spirit, you've got every reason to value it. You get added incentive to clean it up and take care of it. You get a better sense of what you ought to be doing with it.

You can celebrate the reality that wherever you are, the Holy Spirit is with you and in you and for you. Every place you go gets the benefit of the Holy Spirit's presence because you are there. Every person you meet meets the Holy Spirit in you. Everything you do has the potential to be a sacred event because the Holy Spirit is involved in everything you do.

"Your body is the temple of the Holy Spirit," Paul says, *"so glorify God in your body."*

Your body—His temple.

❧

Acts 2:1-21 ESV

¹ When the day of Pentecost arrived, they were all together in one place.
*² And suddenly there came from heaven a sound like a mighty rushing wind,
and it filled the entire house where they were sitting. ³ And divided tongues as
of fire appeared to them and rested on each one of them. ⁴ And they were all
filled with the Holy Spirit and began to speak in other tongues as the Spirit
gave them utterance.*

*⁵ Now there were dwelling in Jerusalem Jews, devout men from every nation
under heaven. ⁶ And at this sound the multitude came together, and they were
bewildered, because each one was hearing them speak in his own language.
⁷ And they were amazed and astonished, saying, "Are not all these who are
speaking Galileans? ⁸ And how is it that we hear, each of us in his own native
language? ⁹ Parthians and Medes and Elamites and residents of Mesopotamia,
Judea and Cappadocia, Pontus and Asia, ¹⁰ Phrygia and Pamphylia, Egypt
and the parts of Libya belonging to Cyrene, and visitors from Rome, ¹¹ both
Jews and proselytes, Cretans and Arabians—we hear them telling in our own
tongues the mighty works of God." ¹² And all were amazed and perplexed,
saying to one another, "What does this mean?" ¹³ But others mocking said,
"They are filled with new wine."*

*¹⁴ But Peter, standing with the eleven, lifted up his voice and addressed
them: "Men of Judea and all who dwell in Jerusalem, let this be known to you,
and give ear to my words. ¹⁵ For these people are not drunk, as you suppose,
since it is only the third hour of the day. ¹⁶ But this is what was uttered through
the prophet Joel:*

> *¹⁷ "And in the last days it shall be, God declares,*
> *that I will pour out my Spirit on all flesh,*
> *and your sons and your daughters shall prophesy,*
> *and your young men shall see visions,*
> *and your old men shall dream dreams;*
> *¹⁸ even on my male servants and female servants*
> *in those days I will pour out my Spirit,*
> *and they shall prophesy.*

¹⁹ *And I will show wonders in the heavens above*
   and signs on the earth below,
   blood, and fire, and vapor of smoke;
²⁰ *the sun shall be turned to darkness*
   and the moon to blood,
   before the day of the Lord comes,
   the great and magnificent day.
²¹ *And it shall come to pass*
   that everyone who calls upon the name of the Lord
   shall be saved."

ৰু৽৽

1 Corinthians 12:3b-13 ESV

³ *…no one speaking in the Spirit of God ever says "Jesus is accursed!"*
and no one can say "Jesus is Lord" except in the Holy Spirit.

⁴ *Now there are varieties of gifts, but the same Spirit;* ⁵ *and there are*
varieties of service, but the same Lord; ⁶ *and there are varieties of activities, but*
it is the same God who empowers them all in everyone. ⁷ *To each is given the*
manifestation of the Spirit for the common good. ⁸ *For to one is given through*
the Spirit the utterance of wisdom, and to another the utterance of knowledge
according to the same Spirit, ⁹ *to another faith by the same Spirit, to another*
gifts of healing by the one Spirit, ¹⁰ *to another the working of miracles, to*
another prophecy, to another the ability to distinguish between spirits, to another
various kinds of tongues, to another the interpretation of tongues. ¹¹ *All these*
are empowered by one and the same Spirit, who apportions to each one
individually as he wills.

¹² *For just as the body is one and has many members, and all the members*
of the body, though many, are one body, so it is with Christ. ¹³ *For in one Spirit*
we were all baptized into one body—Jews or Greeks, slaves or free—and all
were made to drink of one Spirit.

ৰু৽৽

25.

All One Spirit

Acts 2:1-21; 1 Corinthians 12:3b-13 ESV

Today you heard two portions of scripture: the classic story of the coming of the Holy Spirit at Pentecost in Acts, Chapter 2; and Paul's discussion of spiritual gifts in 1st Corinthians 12. The story of Pentecost and the pouring out of divine power on the first disciples is by far the more dramatic passage, but what Paul has to say about the Holy Spirit may well be the more important for us to hear at this point in our life together as a church.

It's kind of like comparing a wedding ceremony and the marriage that results from it. The month of June is the heart of the wedding season. Yesterday, thousands of beautiful brides walked down the aisle to be met by their nervous and undeserving grooms. Some of these ceremonies will have been simple affairs, but these days the trend is to make weddings as spectacular as the bridal party can imagine and the parents can pay or borrow for. Have you been to a no-holds-barred, spare-no-expense, knock-your-socks-off wedding recently? If you have, you'll never forget it. And neither will they.

But within minutes, the ceremony is over. Within hours, the whole grand celebration is history. The tuxes are returned, and that gorgeous dress is stored away in some closet. The caterers clean everything up and the next day, the guests wake up and pack up and go back to wherever they came from. It was a remarkable experience, and the honeymoon will go on for a little while, but the important thing now is the marriage that came out of the wedding. The marriage—the ongoing relationship—*that's* the lasting reality bride and groom, husband and wife, have to live with and work with if the wedding is to fulfill its purpose and justify its excitement and expense.

Pentecost was like one of those weddings that knocked their socks off. It was God's no-holds-barred start of His new and permanent relationship with the disciples of Jesus. That mighty rushing wind of God's Spirit filling that prayer room spun that poor little bunch of Christians up like a holy tornado and tossed them out into the streets of Jerusalem where they bowled over the morning multitude of pilgrims who figured these lunatics must still be hung over from last night's party.

"No—sorry—what you're seeing is the miracle of Pentecost— the pouring out of the Holy Spirit with so much power that every one of us is on fire."

And then the party really began, with Peter toasting the Risen Christ, the Church's totally deserving Bridegroom, with so much inspiration that everybody within earshot wanted a dose of whatever Peter and the other Christians were having. It was a day nobody would forget.

But the birth of a church leads to the life of a church. Yes, you've experienced the coming of the Holy Spirit. You've had your Pentecost. Now what? How do you live successfully— victoriously—now that you got what you wanted?

The wedding was wonderful.

Now, how do you make the marriage work?

And that's where Paul comes in.

Paul is going to tell you how you can be a church—a real, honest-to-God, pleasing-to-God, church. And it all starts with that Holy Spirit poured out at Pentecost.

But it doesn't end there, because the Holy Spirit doesn't end there, because the Holy Spirit came for keeps—to Peter and his buddies in Jerusalem—and then to Paul and those proud, problematic Corinthians—and to every church ever started—and now to us.

Paul is doing the church version of marriage counseling with these Corinthians. They were all excited about *becoming* a church, like a bride at a wedding, but they found *being* a church a little harder than they expected—like being married. So Paul is letting them in on the secret: A church cannot survive without the Holy Spirit.

The Holy Spirit is the glue that holds a body of believers together. The Holy Spirit provides the power that moves a church forward and the direction that keeps the members moving forward together. And the Holy Spirit does this by providing "gifts."

Let's go back to the wedding analogy. When word goes out that a wedding is coming up, people respond by giving gifts. The wedding couple sort of tells their friends and family what to give them. They sign up for wedding registries at places that have the things they want. And they hope people will give them the right stuff.

෯෧

In the church, it's different. There are gifts, of course. But they are spiritual gifts; things that belong to the Holy Spirit and are designed exclusively for the benefit of a particular church.

The Holy Spirit gives all the spiritual gifts that a church will receive. The Holy Spirit, not the individual members of the church, decides what gifts will be given. The Holy Spirit decides who will receive what gift. And no matter how many gifts the Holy Spirit gives a church, all the gifts will form a perfect spread of the same pattern; all will match the scheme of the Holy Spirit for that church. All will bear the Maker's "mark."

There will be no unnecessary duplicate gifts, and nothing essential will be missing. Nothing will need to be returned or traded for something more appropriate or desirable. Every gift the Holy Spirit gives is of equal value with every other gift He gives, though the members may not realize this fact, especially if they do not understand or appreciate the point of the giving.

According to Paul, the Holy Spirit gives everyone in the church a spiritual gift—everyone. And yet, no one gets a gift from the Holy Spirit for his or her own personal benefit.

Every gift that every member of the church is given is for the common good. It's sort of like "community property" in a way—a divine way. To hoard a gift from the Holy Spirit makes no sense, because the only value in the gift is its value to the other members of the church. To flaunt a gift from the Holy Spirit makes even less sense; it was given by the Holy Spirit, with no help from the recipient—and the Holy Spirit doesn't want any of His gifts to be a source of pride.

If it were, the Holy Spirit could quickly and easily take it away.

You see, the Holy Spirit does not give gifts merely for sentimental or aesthetic purposes.

Every spiritual gift has a practical function—a spiritual purpose. Every gift provides an ability to do something a church needs done. And the Holy Spirit knows what that need is, even if the members of the church do not.

For that reason, spiritual gifts that do not make sense are not to be ignored. They are to be exercised so that their purpose and value may be discovered in the process of their use.

❧

Not long ago, this church had one of those knock-your-socks-off spiritual experiences. We felt like brides at a spectacular wedding. Many of us still do. But as the weeks go by and we work at the business of being an honest-to-God, pleasing-to-God church, we start to see a couple of things.

One is all the needs we have that call out for spiritual resources of wisdom, knowledge, faith or miraculous power. The other is all the unexpected spiritual gifts that emerge from people in the process of our being God's church. Not *their* gifts—yours or mine. These gifts are gifts of the Holy Spirit.

The Holy Spirit is equipping this fellowship of ours with everything we need to do His will and be His people. Every success is His success. Every difficulty overcome is His doing. Every miracle is His miracle. Every bond of love and joy and appreciation being built between us here today and in the daily challenges confronting us is the work of the Holy Spirit. All the good things that are happening are the work of the Holy Spirit to Whom we belong by virtue of our faith in Jesus Christ.

I'm not making this stuff up!

Paul says, "All these are the work of one and the same Spirit, and He gives them to each one, just as He determines." All…one…Spirit.

༺⚬⚭༻

As believers, you and I are in Christ, and according to the will of our Lord and Savior, the Holy Spirit has been poured out upon us—let loose among us to meet our needs and make us what God wants us to be. We have been baptized by the Holy Spirit into this church—this Body of Christ. And so we are all one in the Holy Spirit.

We are not merely spectators dazzled for a while by some spectacular but passing event. We are partners by faith and commitment in a permanent relationship with the One Who pours out spiritual gifts upon us, so that we may know the peace that passes understanding,[111] not for an hour or a day, but forever without end. Amen.

༺⚬⚭༻

---

[111] Philippians 4:7.

1 Corinthians 13:1-13 RSV

1 If I speak in the tongues of men and of angels, but have not love, I am a
noisy gong or a clanging cymbal. 2 And if I have prophetic powers, and
understand all mysteries and all knowledge, and if I have all faith, so as to
remove mountains, but have not love, I am nothing. 3 If I give away all I have,
and if I deliver up my body to be burned, but have not love, I gain nothing.

4 Love is patient and kind; love does not envy or boast; it is not arrogant
5 or rude. It does not insist on its own way; it is not irritable or resentful; 6 it
does not rejoice at wrongdoing, but rejoices with the truth. 7 Love bears all
things, believes all things, hopes all things, endures all things.

8 Love never ends. As for prophecies, they will pass away; as for tongues,
they will cease; as for knowledge, it will pass away. 9 For we know in part and
we prophesy in part, 10 but when the perfect comes, the partial will pass away.
11 When I was a child, I spoke like a child, I thought like a child, I reasoned
like a child. When I became a man, I gave up childish ways. 12 For now we see
in a mirror dimly, but then face to face. Now I know in part; then I shall
know fully, even as I have been fully known.

13 So now faith, hope, and love abide, these three; but the greatest of these
is love.

26.

This Thing Called Love

1 Corinthians 13:1-13 RSV

Today, we're going to talk about this thing called "love." The Bible talks about it quite a lot, of course. This 13th chapter of 1st Corinthians may talk about it best.

But we also talk a lot about love. Boy meets girl and finds a hundred way to say, "I love you." We sit down to watch a ball game and discover that you love the Yankees and I love the Braves. You finish a hard day at work and think to yourself: "I'd really love a drink right about now." "Love" can mean a lot of different things to a lot of different people. Today, to narrow the focus, let's talk about this thing the Bible calls love.

The Bible talks about things like family and friendship and romance and sexuality. And the term "love" is certainly applied to the desires and emotions involved in each of these relationships. But Paul here—and the Bible in general—talk about something I want to call "godly love."

Now it's possible that all these other types of love could be subsets under godly love, but experience suggests that they can also be totally separate categories, completely unrelated to any love related to God. Maybe after we look at this thing called godly love,

Biblical love, Christian love, you can figure out where your other loves fit in with it.

You may be interested to know that, according to Paul, godly love doesn't seem to be an emotion or feeling. Of course, the Gospels say, repeatedly, that *"Jesus had compassion on them...."*[112] Wasn't that feeling "love"?

For Paul, the definition of love, even the love of Jesus, is in the *doing*. Perhaps what Jesus *did* as a result of that compassion was the love, for Jesus always did something loving as a result of His compassion. Or perhaps it was this godly love that *generated* His compassion in the first place.

Love is certainly a powerful thing, whether human or divine. Our loves motivate us to propose marriages and purchase merchandise of all kinds. Our loves make us do a lot of wonderful—and wacky—things. And you would expect that God's love, by definition, would be greater—better—than anything we could come up with ourselves.

So what is this godly love the Bible tells us about?

Is it a power?

৯•৩

Paul refers in Philippians to *"...incentive in love...."*[113] This suggests that godly love is the power that motivates godly attitudes and actions. Perhaps this godly love is the power of God that allows us to be connected to God in the only way acceptable to Him, and to connect to other people in the way God intends for those connections to be made. Perhaps this power of godly love is like a tool—or like some equipment God gives us to help us live the life of a Christian.

Let me suggest an analogy to you. Godly love is like a form of spiritual scuba gear that enables you and me to live and function in

---

[112] Matthew 9:36; 14:14; Mark 6:34; Luke 7:13.
[113] Philippians 2:1, RSV.

a realm completely alien to our own. It is like an apparatus that allows us to enter and exist in God's divine world when nothing in our own abilities is adequate.

Or try this: Godly love is not just spiritual survival gear; it is also God's powerful secret weapon in His war to destroy the tyranny of sin and liberate humanity from the occupation forces of evil. After all, the Bible talks openly about spiritual warfare. Paul says in Ephesians: *"...put on the whole armor of God...for we are not contending against flesh and blood, but against...the spiritual hosts of wickedness...."*[114]

❧

And who are the warriors in this spiritual warfare?

Why, the ones to whom God has issued the spiritual weapons.

Paul says in Romans that *"...God's love has been poured into our hearts through the Holy Spirit which has been given to us."*[115]

That's why we sing (or used to sing):

> "Onward Christian soldiers, marching as to war;
> with the Cross of Jesus going on before....
> At the sign of triumph, Satan's host doth flee;
> On, then, Christian soldiers, on to victory!"[116]

Every Christian—*every* Christian—has been given this spiritual scuba gear, this spiritual warfare weapon. So let me ask you: If our spiritual life depends on this equipment every minute of every day—if the difference between victory and defeat in every spiritual battle depends on our effective use of this weapon—shouldn't we be studying it carefully, and learning its capabilities and the requirements for its proper operation and maintenance. Perhaps we should read the instructions provided by the Manufacturer— and commit key sections to memory. After all, in a tough spot,

---

[114] Ephesians 6:11-12, RSV.

[115] Romans 5:5, RSV.

[116] Sabine Baring-Goud and Author Sullivan, "Onward Christian Soldiers," 1865.

every diver—every warrior—knows you may not have time to review the manual. Sometimes the proper procedure has to be instinctive, but instinctively right.

෨⊷ঌ

Well, Paul—a certified expert—is about to hold training on godly love. Like a good instructor, he's going to break it down into its component parts so you can see what they are and how they fit together. So pay attention! You will be tested on this—probably later today and every day for the rest of your life.

Paul starts his class by demonstrating some of the things that might look like godly love, but aren't. You may be surprised at what he dumps into the not-godly-love category. The first thing he sets aside is special speaking talent, whether in the form of eloquence or tongues.

The day before yesterday, I went to hear Alan Keyes speak at William and Mary, the college down the road. Hundreds in the auditorium were enthralled by his eloquence on the importance of moral commitment to the preservation of our freedom and the shaping of our politics. Such eloquence is a wonderful gift.

But the power to move people with words can be abused, as Adolph Hitler proved. It can be abused even in the name of God, as Jimmy Swaggert and others have demonstrated in more recent times.

Nor can speaking in tongues be taken as any sure sign of spiritual superiority. Paul knows of those who speak in tongues without the love of God in their hearts. There were then, and are still today, many who speak in unknown tongues in the practice of religions far removed from Christianity. Apart from godly love, speaking in unknown tongues is impressive, but spiritually empty at the same time.

෨⊷ঌ

And what about people who can predict the future? And what about those with deep, theological insight? And what about those who know the Bible inside and out, backward and forward? And what about those who seem to make the impossible happen?

You can apparently do all these things without love. And without love, all these things are empty of God and worthless to God. The sum total of spiritual benefit gained is zero. These great, awesome religious activities are not love; they may not even signal the presence of love—godly love.

But surely sacrifice and suffering for a worthy cause are examples of this love. Paul says, *"Though I give away all that I have and deliver up my body to be burned, if I have not love, I gain nothing."*

๛

In the recent movie, *Saving Private Ryan*,[117] a squad of soldiers "gave away all they had and delivered up their bodies" to save one particular soldier, one man among tens of thousands in danger, and a stranger to them all. The obvious question that drives the movie is: Will they find him in time to save him?

Yet there is a less obvious, but equally important question: Will they come to care about this young man they are ordered to save? Will they come to love him enough to give their lives for him? Because if they do not, there will be no heroism in their sacrifice, no honor in their suffering.

If they have not love for Private Ryan, they gain nothing.

The nobility is in the power of the love that motivates their sacrifice, not in the sacrifice itself.

Then what, for crying out loud, is godly love? And how do you know it when you see it?

Well, Paul has laid out a dozen separate pieces for you. When you put them all together, you've got a powerful tool, essential equipment, the supreme weapon: God's love.

---

[117] Movie *Saving Private Ryan*, 1998.

Love is patient and kind.
Love is not jealous or boastful.
Love is not arrogant or rude.
Love does not insist on its own way.
Love is not irritable or resentful.
Love does not rejoice at wrong.
Love rejoices in the right.
Love bears all things.
Love believes all things.
Love hopes all things.
Love endures all things.
Love never ends.

❧

So there you have it: the Mark 1, Mod 0, Standard Issue, love of God, fully loaded and operational.

The practice range is open. And as Paul says, *"Make love your aim."*

❧

27.

Becoming a Man

1 Corinthians 13:11 RSV

When I became a man, I put away childish things.

ঌ৹ঌ

It is customary on Father's Day to say good things about good fathers and to encourage all fathers to do a better job.

So, congratulations, Dad, on your good work! Keep it up!

That concludes our customary Father's Day message.

ঌ৹ঌ

I do not intend to talk further to the fathers here today—or to the wives and mothers who have, no doubt, been the secret to much of our success. I want to talk to those of you who will become fathers. And, as always, the rest of you may listen in or nap quietly as you see fit.

Why do I want to talk to the future fathers?

Well, I've found that it is easier and better to prepare properly before time for some great endeavor to come than to attempt after the fact to correct the mistakes that are sure to come from poor or nonexistent preparation. I want to talk to you now because now is the time for you future fathers to get ready for what lies before you.

I want to talk to you about being a father, but I want to talk more about something even more basic: becoming a man.

"What's the big deal about becoming a man?" you may ask. "You just grow up, right?"

Yes, we grow up physically. The body matures automatically.

But to become a man requires more than marking days off a calendar and counting up the years. You enter into manhood by intentional actions and voluntary choices, or you remain in the realm of childhood, regardless your age.

It is an exciting thing to reach the point in your life when the privileges and opportunities of manhood are yours for the taking. In many ways, manhood is the fulfillment of countless boyhood hopes and dreams. But it is a scary thing, too, to become a man and assume a man's obligations and responsibilities.

And yet, something is very wrong when a boy does not want to become a man—when he puts it off unnecessarily. Far too many have chosen this route in our day, and our society is poorer for it.

What's so important about becoming a man?

For one thing, our society is unraveling for lack of godly men. The fabric of our families is coming apart, too—and not just at the seams. There is no "adult supervision" in more and more places. In the absence of men, the immature fill the vacuum and construct a world fit only for their immaturity—and it won't even be fit for that very long. Your family (past and future), your community, your country and your church need you to step up to your responsibilities as a man.

Children need fathers and they need those fathers to be men. Too many of those fathering children in our world today are not man enough to be fathers to those children. To be a father, you must be a man—and here I am specifically not talking biologically.

Oh, you can cause a woman—or a girl—to become pregnant, but that doesn't mean you're a man. In fact, if the woman is not your wife, it means that you are not a man—that you are less than a man. You are just "male." The male of just about every species has that basic physical capacity.

For those of you who will become fathers, it is better in every way that you become men first. You were designed by God to become men. Your purpose in life can only be fulfilled if you will become the men God intends for you to be. Then you can become the fathers God will enable you to be.

What are some of the characteristics of a man?

A man will choose carefully the mother who will bear his children—and will ensure that no one but the right woman will have the opportunity to bear his children. Despite the world's passionate, almost hysterical, assertions to the contrary, a man can do this.

A man will also not put himself in a position to produce children until he is able to support them and their mother financially. He will take the best care he possibly can of the woman who will bear and take care of his children. And needless to say, a man will not destroy his own children. Nor will he encourage the woman bearing them to do so.

A man will not neglect to teach his children spiritual truth. He will not say, "They can decide for themselves what they want to believe when the time comes," because Proverbs 22:6 says, *"Train a child in the way he should go, and when he is old he will not turn from it."*[118] And a man will not wait to figure out what to teach his children about spiritual things when the time comes to teach them. He will figure that out well ahead of time.

A man will tell his children the truth—God's honest truth— because children will believe what their father tells them—until they learn that he does not tell the truth. Then they will never truly believe him again.

---

[118] Proverbs 22:6, RSV.

The conceiving of a child—and especially the birth of one—will focus a man's attention in a powerful way on a father's responsibilities. But the code by which the father fulfills his sacred duties to his children is developed and rehearsed in other relationships long before the establishment of his family.

A man will subordinate his personal agenda so that he can promote the agenda of his family. He will *subordinate* his personal agenda; he will not surrender it entirely.

A man's values and commitments will say more about the meaning and quality of his life than his accomplishments will. And there is no more God-like thing a man can do than to love the children formed in his likeness, and give himself sacrificially for them. After all, your children do not—will not—belong to you. They belong, always and forever, to God.

So what's involved in becoming a man?

The Apostle Paul wrote: *"When I was a child, I spoke as a child, I understood as a child, I thought as a child: but when I became a man, I put away childish things."* [119] That's the old King James wording. And today, it will serve us just fine.

To become a man, you must put away some things—childish things.

కిల్లి

Let's make a distinction here between "childish" and "childlike." Our faith in and obedience to God are to be childlike—completely trusting and confident in God's call and care. That's why Jesus said, *"unless you…become like children you will never enter the kingdom of heaven."* [120]

Unfortunately, as we get older, we are all too quick to trade our childlike faith and character for a cynical, calculating spirit. Jesus

---

[119] 1 Corinthians 13:10-11, KJV.
[120] Matthew 18:3, RSV.

was and remained childlike in His dependence on His Heavenly Father, and this made Him more mature, not less.

To be childish, on the other hand, is to be self-focused and greedy, quick to anger and easily frightened. It is childish to be determined to have all your wants satisfied regardless of the cost to and impact on others. Childishness actively avoids responsibilities and rebels against restrictions—even when they are appropriate.

Have you become a man yet? Would you like to?

If you are thinking that you weren't prepared very well for this transition by the family you grew up in or the life you have led thus far, don't let that deter you. Becoming a man is not about where you've come from; it's about where you propose to go.

Theodore Roosevelt, Jr., the son of the President, was the first Allied general to wade ashore on a Normandy beachhead on D-Day. He landed with the first wave of his army division—in the wrong place on Utah Beach. Roosevelt considered his situation and decided, "We'll start the war from right here!"[121]

Regardless of where life has deposited you today, you can become a man from here. God will make a man out of you, if you let Him.

るふ

"When I became a man, I put away childish things."

What are the childish things you have to put away to become a man?

In general, they are attitudes, actions—and associations—that promote or prolong social, emotional and moral immaturity. They are attitudes that devalue women and ridicule commitment.

---

[121] Stephen E. Ambrose, *D-Day, June 6, 1944: The Climactic Battle of World War II.* New York, NY: Simon & Schuster, 1994, p. 279. See also William C. Meadows, *The Comanche Code Talkers of World War II.* Austin, TX: University of Texas Press, 2002, p. 141.

They are actions that gratify your ego at the expense of others and require others to assume responsibilities that are rightfully yours. They are associations with people who reject Christian values and revel in their extended adolescence, tempting you to do the same. If this description is too nebulous—too theoretical—I can offer more practical examples of what I mean.

For instance, if you would become a man, pull up your pants and tuck in your shirt. Turn your ball cap around and your stereo down.

Do I tell you this because I'm too old to appreciate the current fashion and cultural norms of young people?

Yes and no.

Yes, I am too old to appreciate them, but that's not the issue. These are symbols of an aggressive, belligerent determination not to grow up, and anyone old enough to become a man is too old to be associated with them.

And those who are not yet old enough to become a man will find that the attitudes these symbols stimulate and the associations they promote will make it harder to enter manhood, not easier, when the time comes.

Droopy drawers and blaring music are childish things. And part of becoming a man is putting them away. And so it is with all things childish that hinder the transition into manhood for you.

A final word: Not all men will be fathers, but all men can and should live as though they are, for all of us are children formed in God's likeness—young and old—and every man may offer a father's love to a child of God who needs it. Though every man will not be a father, every child who becomes a man may be a father figure, if he puts away childish things and lives his life in imitation of the Father Who is in Heaven.[122]

ॐॐ

---

[122] Matthew 6:9.

1 Corinthians 15:1-22 ESV

¹ Now I would remind you, brothers, of the gospel I preached to you, which you received, in which you stand, ² and by which you are being saved, if you hold fast to the word I preached to you—unless you believed in vain.

³ For I delivered to you as of first importance what I also received: that Christ died for our sins in accordance with the Scriptures, ⁴ that he was buried, that he was raised on the third day in accordance with the Scriptures, ⁵ and that he appeared to Cephas, then to the twelve. ⁶ Then he appeared to more than five hundred brothers at one time, most of whom are still alive, though some have fallen asleep. ⁷ Then he appeared to James, then to all the apostles. ⁸ Last of all, as to one untimely born, he appeared also to me. ⁹ For I am the least of the apostles, unworthy to be called an apostle, because I persecuted the church of God. ¹⁰ But by the grace of God I am what I am, and his grace toward me was not in vain. On the contrary, I worked harder than any of them, though it was not I, but the grace of God that is with me. ¹¹ Whether then it was I or they, so we preach and so you believed.

¹² Now if Christ is proclaimed as raised from the dead, how can some of you say that there is no resurrection of the dead? ¹³ But if there is no resurrection of the dead, then not even Christ has been raised. ¹⁴ And if Christ has not been raised, then our preaching is in vain and your faith is in vain. ¹⁵ We are even found to be misrepresenting God, because we testified about God that he raised Christ, whom he did not raise if it is true that the dead are not raised. ¹⁶ For if the dead are not raised, not even Christ has been raised. ¹⁷ And if Christ has not been raised, your faith is futile and you are still in your sins. ¹⁸ Then those also who have fallen asleep in Christ have perished. ¹⁹ If in Christ we have hope in this life only, we are of all people most to be pitied.

²⁰ But in fact Christ has been raised from the dead, the firstfruits of those who have fallen asleep. ²¹ For as by a man came death, by a man has come also the resurrection of the dead. ²² For as in Adam all die, so also in Christ shall all be made alive.

☙❧

John 20:19-31 ESV

¹⁹ *On the evening of that day, the first day of the week, the doors being locked where the disciples were for fear of the Jews, Jesus came and stood among them and said to them, "Peace be with you." ²⁰ When he had said this, he showed them his hands and his side. Then the disciples were glad when they saw the Lord. ²¹ Jesus said to them again, "Peace be with you. As the Father has sent me, even so I am sending you." ²² And when he had said this, he breathed on them and said to them, "Receive the Holy Spirit. ²³ If you forgive the sins of any, they are forgiven them; if you withhold forgiveness from any, it is withheld."*

²⁴ *Now Thomas, one of the twelve, called the Twin, was not with them when Jesus came. ²⁵ So the other disciples told him, "We have seen the Lord." But he said to them, "Unless I see in his hands the mark of the nails, and place my finger into the mark of the nails, and place my hand into his side, I will never believe."*

²⁶ *Eight days later, his disciples were inside again, and Thomas was with them. Although the doors were locked, Jesus came and stood among them and said, "Peace be with you." ²⁷ Then he said to Thomas, "Put your finger here, and see my hands; and put out your hand, and place it in my side. Do not disbelieve, but believe." ²⁸ Thomas answered him, "My Lord and my God!" ²⁹ Jesus said to him, "Have you believed because you have seen me? Blessed are those who have not seen and yet have believed."*

³⁰ *Now Jesus did many other signs in the presence of the disciples, which are not written in this book; ³¹ but these are written so that you may believe that Jesus is the Christ, the Son of God, and that by believing you may have life in his name.*

৵৽৹

28.

For Want of a Resurrection...

1 Corinthians 15:1-22; John 20:19-31 ESV

There is a nursery rhyme that has been around for hundreds of years (in one form or another) that traces a massive disaster back to a seemingly insignificant detail. The initial, insignificant detail is the loss of a horseshoe nail. But this minor inconvenience causes other, cascading problems—and before you know it—without imagining it possible—the greatest catastrophe befalls.

One version of the verse goes like this:

> For want of a nail the shoe was lost.
> For want of a shoe the horse was lost.
> For want of a horse the rider was lost.
> For want of a rider the battle was lost.
> For want of a victory the kingdom was lost.
> And all for the want of a nail.[123]

The kingdom was lost—all for the want of a nail.

Now, hold that thought—we'll come back to it.

ॐ•ॐ

---

[123] Quoted by Benjamin Franklin in *Poor Richard's Almanac* in 1758.

Chapter 15 of 1ˢᵗ Corinthians is no nursery rhyme, but the Apostle Paul is engaged in a little "one thing leads to another" discussion in its verses. He begins, not with the loss of a horseshoe nail, but with an unwillingness of some people to believe something—the unwillingness of some of the Christians in the Corinthian church to believe in the resurrection of the dead.

You wouldn't think that what a group of people believes—or doesn't believe—would be that important. It's just an idea—an attitude—a perspective. And we're not talking about a lot of people—or anybody very important, in the grand scheme of things. At least, that's how it seems.

But to hear Paul tell it, a lot more than a kingdom will be lost—all for the want of a belief in the resurrection of the dead: *"…if there is no resurrection of the dead, then not even Christ has been raised. And if Christ has not been raised, then our preaching is in vain and your faith is in vain…. We are…misrepresenting God…the dead are not raised…and you are still in your sins."*

∾

A lot of people today don't believe in the idea of a resurrection from the dead—not for Jesus—not for anybody. It's an idea that just doesn't sit well with the empirical mindset that emerged in the Age of Reason. It doesn't make sense in this modern world when powerful space telescopes can't find heaven and cutting-edge CAT scans can map your body but miss your soul.

The world around us is systematically dismantling all the evidence of the witnesses of the Resurrection of Jesus. Sacred words are erased from civic buildings, prohibited from being there by law. Public expressions of faith in the Resurrection are also banned from societal gatherings, and private expressions are viciously attacked as hateful and harmful to the common good.

Even in the broad community of individuals who still identify themselves as Christians, more and more folks are concluding that identifying themselves with the idea of a bodily resurrection is intellectually indefensible and theologically unnecessary. Many who maintain an affiliation with a church today do so merely to promote some generic form of good behavior and to enjoy the emotional and commercial benefits of some occasional religious activity. Their approach? Embrace what you feel comfortable with in the biblical witness about Jesus and distance yourself (quietly or otherwise) from the rest.

To the world, the Resurrection isn't really that important. To the world, it isn't real at all. It's a fairy tale no more significant or relevant to life than a nail from a horse's shoe.

"People aren't resurrected. Resurrections don't happen. That's not how the world works."

Today, people know better than the Bible, it seems.

But don't be too fast in ascribing this attitude just to the infinitely greater sophistication of the *modern* mind. They were saying this sort of stuff—in churches—within decades of the Resurrection itself, while plenty of eyewitnesses were still around to confirm they had seen Jesus alive after His Crucifixion. People were "putting down" the Resurrection in the church in Corinth within months (or weeks?) of Paul himself sharing the gospel of salvation with them, including, no doubt, his own testimony of his personal encounter with the Risen Christ.

Wanting to wriggle out of believing the Resurrection is nothing new. As Paul's argument indicates, Christians were already trying to dismiss the Resurrection before most of the books in the New Testament had been written.

And ever since, there have been two kinds of people in the world: those who do not believe in the Resurrection—and those who do...

...which brings us back to the nursery rhyme about the horseshoe nail.

Those people—in the church and out—who do *not* believe in the Resurrection are living their lives amid a process not unlike the one described in the children's tale. They are missing something.

To them, it seems like nothing—completely insignificant. But because they do not believe in the Resurrection—because they do not "have" the Resurrection as a part of their lives—they do not have something else.

They do not have the power of the living Christ available to—and active in—their lives. After all, if you do not believe that Jesus has been raised from the dead, you're not going to believe that He is alive now. And you're not really going to believe that He can love you or protect you or guide you as you go about the business of living your life each day.

All you can do is wrap your thoughts, your decisions, your values and your actions in a mantle of "Christian respectability." All you have is *your* power, or that of other people—*your* wisdom, or that of other people—*your* sense of right and wrong, or that of the people around you. But for want of the Resurrection, the Risen Christ is lost to you. All you're left with is whatever religious fervor or feelings you can generate on your own or with the help of those other people.

And for want of the Risen Christ, a genuine, living relationship with Him is lost to you. And if you have no relationship with the living Christ, the power He would give you is lost to you as well. And if you cannot receive His power, you cannot know the hope that comes from it. And if you lack the divine hope that grows out of your experiencing the power of the Risen Christ, you lose out on the peace that passes understanding[124] and the joy that knows no end.[125]

How did Paul put it?

"…if there is no resurrection of the dead…your faith is in vain."

But that's not all.

"…if there is no resurrection of the dead…you are still in your sins."

---

[124] Philippians 4:7.
[125] John 16:22-24.

For want of the Resurrection, you have no assurance of salvation—no *hope* of salvation.

When the nail was lost, it triggered a chain reaction that ended in the loss of an earthy kingdom. For want of faith in the Resurrection, the end-result is your losing the glorious place that could have been yours—*would* have been yours—in the eternal kingdom of God.

☙❧

On the other hand, there are those silly, misguided, dim-witted people who *do* believe in the Resurrection of the dead today—people like—well—you and me.

If you believe, as the Bible teaches, that God raised Jesus from the dead—so that Jesus lives forever as the eternal King of kings—your faith is not in theological ideas, but in a living Person. Because you believe Jesus lives, you are open to His divine, redemptive interaction with you. Because you are open in faith to the involvement of the living Lord in your life, you experience the impact of His active power in your life.

This miraculous power you experience gives you a reason and the confidence to hope in His promises to bless you and keep you, in this life and the next. Being able to believe that the living Jesus has saved you from the condemnation of sin by His death and is sustaining you—forever—by His infinite power and love, makes incredible joy possible, whatever the burdens this life may bring.

You're looking at two totally different kinds of life when you compare the person who believes in the Resurrection with the person who doesn't. If you don't believe me, look at Thomas, the Apostle, before and after He saw the Risen Christ.

For a week after the Resurrection, Thomas did not believe Jesus had been raised, even though the other disciples assured him it was so. For a week, Jesus remained dead to Thomas.

Thomas had no sense of the power of the Resurrection. He was closed to the power of Jesus. He had no hope. He had no joy.

He was dead inside because he could not believe that Jesus was *not* dead. That was his life—for a week.

And then, Thomas saw Jesus—alive. Thomas became one who had not believed the Resurrection and then did. His darkness turned to light. His helplessness was replaced with power. His hopelessness evaporated, and joy poured in to take its place.

In the upper room at the Last Supper, Thomas had complained to the soon-to-be-crucified Jesus, *"Lord, we do not know where you are going. How can we know the way?"*[126] In this locked-up room with the Risen Jesus, Thomas knows immediately everything he needs to know. His life has just gone from "over" to over-joyed: *"My Lord and my God!"*

Everything he thought he had lost when he did not believe in the Resurrection, Thomas discovered that he gained the moment he did believe in it.

"But Thomas *saw* Jesus. And Paul *saw* Jesus. The eyewitnesses all *saw* Jesus, raised from the dead."

And if you believe in the Resurrection, you will, too. You will see the impact of His power *in* your life. You will see the influence of His love *on* your life. You will see the miracles of His grace *throughout* your life. You will see the confirmation of your faith in ways the world (and maybe even you) cannot understand. You will see His kingdom coming and your place in it—a place you had lost because of your sin and regained because of your faith in the One Who died to restore it to you.

If you believe in the Resurrection, you will be a witness to it. You will see Jesus, time and time again—alive—resurrected and reigning. If you "nail down" your belief in the resurrection of the dead—and the Resurrection of Jesus Christ—all that might have been lost to you will be safe and secured forever.

ॐ⋖

---

126 John 14:5, ESV.

From the 2nd Letter to the Corinthians

2 Corinthians 4:7-18 ESV

⁷ But we have this treasure in jars of clay, to show that the surpassing power belongs to God and not to us. ⁸ We are afflicted in every way, but not crushed; perplexed, but not driven to despair; ⁹ persecuted, but not forsaken; struck down, but not destroyed; ¹⁰ always carrying in the body the death of Jesus, so that the life of Jesus may also be manifested in our bodies. ¹¹ For we who live are always being given over to death for Jesus' sake, so that the life of Jesus also may be manifested in our mortal flesh. ¹² So death is at work in us, but life in you.

¹³ Since we have the same spirit of faith according to what has been written, "I believed, and so I spoke," we also believe, and so we also speak, ¹⁴ knowing that he who raised the Lord Jesus will raise us also with Jesus and bring us with you into his presence. ¹⁵ For it is all for your sake, so that as grace extends to more and more people it may increase thanksgiving, to the glory of God.

¹⁶ So we do not lose heart. Though our outer self is wasting away, our inner self is being renewed day by day. ¹⁷ For this light momentary affliction is preparing for us an eternal weight of glory beyond all comparison, ¹⁸ as we look not to the things that are seen but to the things that are unseen. For the things that are seen are transient, but the things that are unseen are eternal.

8o8

29.

But Not Destroyed

2 Corinthians 4:7-18 ESV

The Apostle Paul had some sobering things to say when he wrote to his friends in Corinth:

"...we...are always being given over to death...."

"...death is at work in us...."

"We are afflicted, perplexed,
persecuted, struck down...."

"...our outer self is wasting away...."

And this was his "sales pitch" for Christianity.

And yet Christianity took root in those to whom Paul said these things and others like them. This faith in Jesus took root and grew and has continued to grow for thousands of years in millions of hearts, despite the fact that everything Paul wrote is true.

Most of us know the truth of Paul's words from personal experience. We have said our good-byes as a loved one breathed his last—or hers. We have said our prayers as we prepared to go under the surgeon's knife. We come so quickly to that point in life where we can mark in the mirror the incremental but cumulative wasting away of our outer self.

❧

"Death is at work in us...." And with it, and before it, comes all manner of suffering and sorrow. Paul was talking about what he endured to preach the gospel, but all of us endure some measure of affliction, perplexity and persecution. There is no guarantee that you will not be "struck down" in this life, not even if you're a Christian. You are, as Paul put it, a "jar of clay."

Older translations say, *"earthen vessels."*[127] And it is only a matter of time before a jar of clay collapses—before an earthen vessel returns to the earth from which it came.

But it gets worse.

"We are always being given over," not *"to death...,"* as some versions of the Bible translate it, but *"to the dying..."*—to the daily exposure to danger and disappointment, hardship and suffering that goes on throughout this life. Old Job said, *"...man is born to trouble as the sparks fly upward."*[128] This world can break you in pieces—it can tear you apart—long before it takes your life. You know this—and what it's like—if you've been broken or torn by the ways of the world.

And yet, Paul is not preaching "gloom and doom." He knows everything there is to know about heartache, pain and suffering. But he knows something else that's even more important.

Yes, we are earthen vessels. We are weak and helpless, worthless in the marketplace of the material world.

But Paul knows those who claim Christ have a *treasure* in their earthen vessels.

Christianity, at its core, is a paradox about something priceless contained in something worthless. It's the miracle of the Incarnation: Jesus, a Jewish peasant, a human being, was an "earthen vessel" like anyone else. Yet *"in him, all the fullness of God"*—a priceless treasure—*"was pleased to dwell."*[129] The gospel—the good news of salvation in Jesus Christ—is a priceless treasure

---

[127] See KJV, RSV, NASB, etc.
[128] Job 5:7, RSV.
[129] Colossians 1:19, RSV.

to any who will receive it, even though you and I who claim the good news and convey it to others are, ourselves, insignificant earthen vessels.

For the believer, the dying that we are always being given over to is the dying *of Jesus.*

Our human suffering has become a shared suffering. There is alongside our suffering a life-giving Spirit, sharing our suffering and drawing it up out of the meaningless of this world into the suffering of Christ, so that our suffering—our sickness, sorrow and death—are somehow made a part of the redemptive reality of God and the Savior He sent to free us from this valley of the shadow of death[130]—this vale of tears[131] we cannot otherwise endure or escape.[132]

Blow as the gales of hardship and heartache may in this world, the "pilot light" of spiritual power and peace still burns within us and for us and waits for that moment when it will burst forth in flame to warm us and guide us again. What we experience may break our hearts, but we do not *lose* heart. The world and its woes may wear you down and wring you out till it seems that nothing worthwhile remains. But the weaker you become in the face of your suffering or grief, the stronger the God within you grows.[133]

✂◈

And here's a mystery: Those who suffer most in the company of Christ bestow the most blessing in the wake of what is left. We have this divine treasure in *our* earthen vessels.

When the world does its worst—when your life looks worthless—you may be assured that there is more there than the world counted on—more than *you* counted on—at work in you.

---

[130] Psalm 23:4.
[131] Psalm 84:6, from the Latin Vulgate, Wycliffe's and the Bishops' Bible.
[132] Romans 8:10.
[133] 2 Corinthians 12:9.

You lose "everything" and then in the midst of the "nothing" that is left, you discover: *Something*—a miraculous Something that is not you, but is there, in you, just the same.

Pitiful earthen vessel—and the priceless treasure inside.

When you are *"afflicted...perplexed...persecuted...struck down..."*—and there are times when you will be—there are truths you must know as a Christian, and trust them. There are truths you must know when everything within you tells you that what you *feel* is all there is. And what you feel—all you *can* feel—is empty and alone. What you feel is the end of any chance of happiness ever again—the end of hope for anything other than the present agony that you feel you cannot endure. It's what you *feel*. But it is not the truth—not for an earthen vessel with a treasure inside.

Paul calls this "hell in your heart" a *"light momentary affliction,"* which seems incredibly heartless and cruel of a man of God—until you remember that Paul has been through everything you have—and more. He has experienced the life of daily dying—and he has discovered and depended on the treasure that resides in *his* earthen vessel—as it does in you.

If your greatest afflictions are in any way "lightweight and temporary," they are so only in comparison to something that is truly incomparable: the eternal and infinitely substantial glory of God that will be that priceless thing you trade all your sorrows and suffering—all your pain and despair—for. That's the full measure of God's glory—the experience of *no* pain of any kind forever—and no *possibility* of any—and no *concern* about the possibility of any. God's glory is the experience of the undoing of all that has caused you pain and sorrow, as God makes all things right at last.

The glory to come is not merely God's compassionate compensation for your present suffering. It is that your earthly afflictions, experienced in the context of your Christian faith, form the foundation for the glory to come—glory whose foretaste you are favored enough to enjoy even in the midst of the suffering you must endure here and now.

You must know that what you see of, and in, this world is not all there is, and that what you do not see is infinitely more—and infinitely more wonderful—than what you *do* see.

So let's go back and see the unseen things that Paul would have you see.

ॐ•ॐ

Paul would have you see that the things that are seen—the sufferings clamoring to consume you—are transient, while the unseen things of God's grace are eternal. Paul would have you see that though your outer self is wasting away, your inner self, where the treasure is, is being renewed by that treasure every day.

Everyone is being "given over" to death. It's the way of the world. But you who have given your life and your suffering and your death over to Jesus are always being given over to death—for Jesus' sake. And so your suffering means something very different.

Everything about your life is defined by the death of Jesus— and, therefore, by the life of Jesus—so that your life is not about dying anymore, but about living—like Jesus—in Jesus. An earthen vessel—full of treasure.

And Paul said something else, *"...in Adam, all die."*[134] That's the hopeless way of the world: Earthen vessels are all ultimately destroyed.

Yet there's another way: *"...in Christ shall all be made alive."* Oh, and by the way, he also said, *"the dead in Christ shall rise...to meet Him...."*[135]

The suffering and death of this world will put you down. They will bury you—like worthless earthen vessels. The life of Christ is a life that was dead and has been resurrected—it was given life forever.[136] It is a treasure that transforms earthen vessels.

---

[134] 1 Corinthians 15:22, RSV.
[135] 1 Thessalonians 4:16-17.
[136] Romans 8:11.

"Will there be no afflictions for the vessel with the treasure inside?"

Sorry. There will be afflictions of every kind.

"Will the Christian get a pass on perplexity?"

No. Perplexity is still on the program.

"Can I at least sit out the persecution? "

Not possible.

"Will I be struck down?"

Yes, probably—and so hard sometimes that you won't be able to pick yourself up—and won't want to.

"So what's so wonderful about this treasure within me?"

He will not let the afflictions crush you. He will not let the insanity of life drive you crazy. He will not let you go through persecution alone and unprotected. And no matter what happens, your Lord and Savior will not let you be destroyed.

And when you endure it all with His help—when you survive it all by His grace—you will understand the priceless nature of the treasure you possess in your earthen vessel—your jar of clay. You will understand and thank your God for the treasure that possesses you—and blesses you with His life in the midst of this dying world.

❧

"We have this treasure in earthen vessels, to show that the surpassing power belongs to God and not to us."

Suffering, but not destroyed.

Grieving, but not destroyed.

Numb, but not destroyed.

Inconsolable, but not destroyed.

In spite of everything—because of the surpassing power of God in Jesus Christ—nothing in this world will ever destroy you—if you have this treasure—in you.

❧

2 Corinthians 5:14-21 ESV

¹⁴ For the love of Christ controls us, because we have concluded this: that one has died for all, therefore all have died; ¹⁵ and he died for all, that those who live might no longer live for themselves but for him who for their sake died and was raised.

¹⁶ From now on, therefore, we regard no one according to the flesh. Even though we once regarded Christ according to the flesh, we regard him thus no longer. ¹⁷ Therefore, if anyone is in Christ, he is a new creation. The old has passed away; behold, the new has come. ¹⁸ All this is from God, who through Christ reconciled us to himself and gave us the ministry of reconciliation; ¹⁹ that is, in Christ God was reconciling the world to himself, not counting their trespasses against them, and entrusting to us the message of reconciliation. ²⁰ Therefore, we are ambassadors for Christ, God making his appeal through us. We implore you on behalf of Christ, be reconciled to God. ²¹ For our sake he made him to be sin who knew no sin, so that in him we might become the righteousness of God.

෧ை

Luke 18:9-17 ESV

⁹ *[Jesus] also told this parable to some who trusted in themselves that they were righteous, and treated others with contempt:* ¹⁰ *"Two men went up into the temple to pray, one a Pharisee and the other a tax collector.* ¹¹ *The Pharisee, standing by himself, prayed thus: 'God, I thank you that I am not like other men, extortioners, unjust, adulterers, or even like this tax collector.* ¹² *I fast twice a week; I give tithes of all that I get.'* ¹³ *But the tax collector, standing far off, would not even lift up his eyes to heaven, but beat his breast, saying, 'God, be merciful to me, a sinner!'* ¹⁴ *I tell you, this man went down to his house justified, rather than the other. For everyone who exalts himself will be humbled, but the one who humbles himself will be exalted."*

¹⁵ *Now they were bringing even infants to him that he might touch them. And when the disciples saw it, they rebuked them.* ¹⁶ *But Jesus called them to him, saying, "Let the children come to me, and do not hinder them, for to such belongs the kingdom of God.* ¹⁷ *Truly, I say to you, whoever does not receive the kingdom of God like a child shall not enter it."*

৵৹৶

30.

Reconciliation

2 Corinthians 5:14-21, Luke 18:9-17 ESV

So, here's the picture: two guys—maybe strangers to each other, maybe not—both happened to head to church about the same time. One is unusually well dressed; the other, not so much.

Maybe the place is crowded, and they end up next to each other, though they would rather not be. Everybody is praying out loud, since silent prayer hasn't been invented yet or something, and the two men next to each other are joining in the din with their own personal prayers.

The well-dressed man is well-dressed because he is a tax collector. He can buy the best clothes because he takes what money he wants from his neighbors. The other man clothes himself in the simple, but distinctive, style of the spiritually superior Pharisee. If clothes *don't* make the man, they still can give you a pretty good idea of the kind of man you're dealing with.

The well-dressed man is praying, but it's the other guy, the one in the simple clothes, who's turning up the volume and turning the heads of those around him. And for a personal prayer, he's spending an awful lot of time telling God about the guy next to him. To hear the Pharisee's prayer—and he's going to make sure that everybody within yards will—to hear his prayer, the guy standing next to him in the very good clothes is such a very bad guy he ought to be tossed out of God's House on his ear—or on the seat of his high-priced and well-pressed pants.

But the guy with the impressive suit isn't there to show off his wardrobe. He doesn't seem to be paying any attention to the guy beside him who's paying so much attention to him.

The guy praying loudly next to him isn't too happy about being next to him. But the guy in the good suit doesn't seem to be too happy, either. And the reason seems to be that he has the same opinion of *himself* that the Pharisee beside him has.

The well-dressed guy is going to wrinkle his suit coat because, while he's praying, he keeps hitting himself in the chest. And he keeps repeating, over and over: *"God, be merciful to me, a sinner!"*

The "praying P.A. system" standing next to him is telling God something a bit different, "God, You are so lucky to have a "sin avoider" like me on Your team!"

And then, these two guys—maybe strangers, maybe not—go home after praying their hearts out.

One was begging for reconciliation—one was bellowing for recognition. Both, it turns out, got what they prayed for. But sooner or later, both men will understand that reconciliation with God is a lot better purpose for prayer than the recognition of men.

ॐ⋘

The Apostle Paul had been one of these plain-dressing, proud-praying Pharisees[137] before he got his understanding about prayer and everything else "adjusted" on the Damascus Road.[138]

When Paul (on the way to his appointment to persecute the followers of Christ) encountered the Christ he thought was dead (and found that He was very much alive), Paul experienced a reconciliation with God he didn't even know he needed. Paul's

---

[137] Philippians 3:4-7.
[138] Acts 9:3-6.

relationship with God had been broken when he thought it was perfect.

Then, before he had a chance to beg for mercy, he received mercy. Before he could do anything to make things right with God, God made Paul right with Him.

Paul became the poster child for divine reconciliation. Paul no longer lives for himself.[139] He's no longer impressed with himself.[140] He looks at himself differently. He looks at everybody else differently. He looks at Christ differently because he doesn't have a choice. He met Christ face to face and Christ wasn't dead the way Paul thought He was.

Christ showed Paul how different everything is because of what God did in Christ. And Paul was reconciled. He was reconciled to God, and he concluded that what God did for him in Christ, God did for everybody else in Christ, too. Paul concluded that God was reconciling the whole world to Himself in Christ, and that anyone who was "in Christ" was reconciled to God.

And so he made it his business from then on to get people "in Christ" so that they would, in fact, be reconciled with God. It became his obsession—his ministry. It was his message to a world of people who had no clue they needed to be reconciled to God— or if they did, they had no clue—no correct clue—about how to go about getting reconciled—how it could be accomplished for them...

...which is understandable, since reconciliation is one of the hardest things in the world for anybody to accomplish—with anybody. Paul was reconciled to God, but he was constantly trying to bring about reconciliation with other people. Sometimes, he was mediating between other people, such as Philemon and his runaway slave, Onesimus,[141] or Euodia and Syntyche, two "church

---

[139] Galatians 2:19-20.
[140] 1 Timothy 1:15.
[141] Philemon 1:8-22.

ladies" in the Philippian church who were on the "outs" with each other for some reason.[142]

As often as not, Paul was trying to pull off some reconciliation between himself and some church—or some faction in a church—he himself had founded. That's really what's going on in 2nd Corinthians. The Corinthians have given Paul the cold shoulder and he's trying to work out a reconciliation with them by pointing to the reconciliation he and they have both received from God.

"If God would reconcile us to Himself, can't you—shouldn't you—reconcile me to yourselves? Isn't this what God wants you to do? Isn't this what your reconciliation with God is for?" writes Paul.

But, oh, how hard it is for people to get along—even good, Christian people like us. Oh, we expect it to be hard for nation to be reconciled to nation. We have multitudes of professional diplomats—ambassadors—all around the world, and their best efforts frequently can't even keep the peace, much less make peace when it's been lost. It's hard for individuals—strangers—to get along. It's hard for neighbors. It's hard for schoolmates and siblings and spouses to get along—and harder still to be reconciled when we've had some falling out.

❧

But if I am reconciled to God through the death of Christ—and you are reconciled to God through the death of Christ—can we not be reconciled to one another through the death of Christ as well? Is this not, perhaps, God's will for His children—that reconciliation might be the result in all our relationships?

To hear Paul tell it, reconciliation is our business. It's the job God has given us. Not that we could die on the Cross like Jesus did—not that we could pay the price to reconnect some sinner to God—ourselves or anybody else.

---

[142] Philippians 4:2-3.

But we can tell people about this reconciliation with God. And we can urge people to let God reconcile them to Himself. We can pray prayers for the divine reconciliation of others and prayers that God will reconcile people with each other. And we can recognize that because we have been reconciled to God, God can and does enable us to be reconciled to others.

Have you been reconciled to God?

Then you have been appointed a minister of reconciliation—an ambassador carrying a sacred message of peace to anyone in the world who can't get along with God. To fulfill your mission, you must let God reconcile you with those in your home, your family, your neighborhood, your school or wherever, who are distant, hostile, estranged.

Hard to do?

In many cases, humanly impossible.

ॐ

But suppose those two men who went to pray that day had stood next to each other and prayed the same prayer—not the Pharisee's prayer that put more distance between himself and the man beside him—and the God above him—but the tax collector's prayer, humbling himself to the point that God had to come closer just to hear him make his confession and repent his way to reconciliation.

Jesus said that one man went home justified—another word for reconciled. Two praying the tax collector's prayer would have come away from the experience, not further apart, but united in heart and mind, and pure in spirit—as pure as the little children who came to Jesus to be blessed. We are not those little children, but we are made like them by Christ, as are any we bring to Christ for reconciliation through His death.

Get the message?

Be reconciled to God—and to each other.

ॐ

2 Corinthians 6:1-13 NRSV

[1] *Working together with him, then, we appeal to you not to receive the grace of God in vain.* [2] *For he says,*

> *"In a favorable time I listened to you,*
> *and in a day of salvation I have helped you."*

Behold, now is the favorable time; behold, now is the day of salvation. [3] *We put no obstacle in anyone's way, so that no fault may be found with our ministry,* [4] *but as servants of God we commend ourselves in every way: by great endurance, in afflictions, hardships, calamities,* [5] *beatings, imprisonments, riots, labors, sleepless nights, hunger;* [6] *by purity, knowledge, patience, kindness, the Holy Spirit, genuine love;* [7] *by truthful speech, and the power of God; with the weapons of righteousness for the right hand and for the left;* [8] *through honor and dishonor, through slander and praise. We are treated as impostors, and yet are true;* [9] *as unknown, and yet well known; as dying, and behold, we live; as punished, and yet not killed;* [10] *as sorrowful, yet always rejoicing; as poor, yet making many rich; as having nothing, yet possessing everything.*

[11] *We have spoken freely to you, Corinthians; our heart is wide open.* [12] *You are not restricted by us, but you are restricted in your own affections.* [13] *In return (I speak as to children) widen your hearts also.*

৯৶৶

31.

With Weapons of Righteousness

2 Corinthians 6:1-13 NRSV

In the sixth chapter of 2nd Corinthians, the Apostle Paul is laying out the case for the legitimacy of his spiritual leadership. He counts off the kinds of difficulties he has endured in the service of Christ: *"beatings, imprisonments…hunger."* He describes the way he has conducted himself: with *"purity, patience, kindness and love."*

And then Paul offers a most arresting description of himself: *"with weapons of righteousness for the right hand and for the left."* So this is how Paul sees himself: a warrior in the service of his King.

The parade of images and arguments flows on, but we will stop here for a while and inspect this particular image a little more closely: *"with weapons of righteousness for the right hand and the left."*

❧

In New Testament times, the Roman Empire ruled the world by the might of its military—the power and prowess of its soldiers. And Paul would have been no stranger to these warriors and their weapons since Paul was, at different times, both a free Roman citizen and a prisoner in their charge. It would be natural for Paul to draw upon that image of the Roman soldier to describe his own role in the cosmic battle between the forces of evil and the Risen Christ.

"Our struggle," Paul says in a different place, *"is not against flesh and blood, but against the rulers, against the authorities, against the powers of this dark world and against the spiritual forces of evil in the heavenly realms."*[143]

Later in 2nd Corinthians, in Chapter 10, Paul will describe the nature of the weapons involved in this struggle: *"The weapons we fight with are not the weapons of the world. On the contrary, they have divine power to demolish strongholds. We demolish arguments and every pretension that sets itself up against the knowledge of God, and we take captive every thought to make it obedient to Christ"*[144]—with the weapons of righteousness.

ॐ

But Paul is more specific than that here: *"with weapons of righteousness—for the right hand and for the left."*

What, specifically, are those weapons?

Those who saw Roman soldiers everyday would immediately understand. The right hand was the strong hand—the offensive hand—the hand that bore the weapon of attack. In his right hand, a warrior carried a sword.

With his left hand, he defended himself. With his left hand, the warrior carried a shield.

And so the weapons *"for the right hand and for the left"* are sword and shield.

But what are the spiritual versions of sword and shield? What are the *"weapons of righteousness for the right hand and the left"*?

To answer this question, we have to go to the "spiritual armory" located in the Book of Ephesians. There Paul says: *"Put on the full armor of God so that you can take your stand against the devil's*

---

[143] Ephesians 6:12, NIV.
[144] 2 Corinthians 10:4-5, NIV.

schemes...so that when the day of evil comes, you may be able to stand your ground."[145]

And then Paul gives a tour of the armory: belt of truth, breastplate of righteousness, helmet of salvation. The armory contains a sword and a shield as well,[146] the *"weapons of righteousness for the right hand and the left."*

But this is not a museum, some dusty display of relics. This is a working armory. Paul is issuing state-of-the-art equipment, designed, crafted and supplied by the Commander-in-Chief Himself. It is state-of-the-art weaponry, and it is standard issue for all those who serve as warriors in the ranks of the redeemed.

ॐ

First, there is your shield: *"...take up the shield of faith,"* Paul says, *"with which you can extinguish all the flaming arrows of the evil one...."*[147] The weapon of righteousness for your left hand—for your defense—is the shield of faith.

In Paul's day, a warrior's shield was a priceless possession. He protected it and preserved it when he was not in battle so that it would protect and preserve him when the battle was joined. He passed it on to his descendants.

A warrior attended to his shield constantly, anointing its leather covering with oil so that it would not become dry, brittle and weak. A strong shield was the difference between life and death—victory and defeat—for the warrior on the battlefield.

When the flaming arrows of the evil one rain down on you, it will be your faith in Jesus that will save you from the devastation of heart and mind and spirit all these terrible things would wreak upon you. Not your intellect or your bank account, not your social connections, your good looks or your good name—only your faith. And if your faith is not strong, your defense may not be adequate.

---

145 Ephesians 6:11, 13, RSV.
146 Ephesians 6:14-17.
147 Ephesians 6:16, ESV.

Faith is a powerful weapon of righteousness—our sure and certain defense—but only if we hold it properly. The shield of the Roman soldier, as Paul knew from personal experience, was not held loosely or at arm's length. It was equipped with more than a single handle (from which the shield might be ripped away in the storm of battle).

The Roman shield was an effective means of defense because it had two handles. The first, the warrior slipped his entire left arm through, so that he could hold his shield close to his body—over his head and next to his heart—making it as much a part of himself as possible.

With his left hand, he grasped the second handle with all his might so that nothing in the heat of battle could separate him from the shield that preserved him.

The shield of faith-in-Jesus-Christ is the weapon of righteousness that God has issued you for your defense. But even superior, state-of-the-art equipment will not protect you if is not maintained properly and used in combat as intended. You must attend to your faith and nurture it every chance you get. You must hold it close and make it as much a part of you as you possibly can—if it is to protect and preserve you as God intends.

સ્જૅ

That being said, wars are not won by defense—by merely avoiding defeat.[148] And God is not content merely to defend those He has called to faith in Jesus Christ. God sent Jesus to overcome the world of sin and death[149]—to launch such an assault that all the forces of evil combined cannot withstand it.[150]

---

[148] See Winston Churchill's speech of June 4, 1940, after the near miraculous rescue of British forces from the French port of Dunkirk,: "Wars are not won by evacuations."
[149] John 16:33.
[150] Matthew 16:18.

The purpose of God is not to *preserve* His kingdom. God has formed His mighty army under the banner of Christ to *advance* His kingdom[151]—into every dark corner of every human heart and wherever the supernatural enemies of His righteousness resist.

And for that reason, there is an offensive weapon of righteousness for the *right* hand of God's warriors. Back in the spiritual armory, Paul says, *"Take…the sword of the Spirit, which is the word of God."*[152]

The writer of Hebrews describes it this way: *"…the word of God is living and active. Sharper than any double-edged sword, it penetrates even to dividing soul and spirit, joints and marrow; it judges the thoughts and attitudes of the heart."*[153]

Defended by our faith in Jesus, we advance into a hostile world with the Word of God. And, in truth, it is the Word of God that demolishes *"…arguments and every pretension that sets itself up against the knowledge of God."* It is the Word of God that takes *"captive every thought…."*[154] We merely wield the weapon—the right-hand weapon of righteousness. And we must wield it, with courage and confidence and skill.

What warrior, after all, goes into battle unarmed? What warrior goes into battle without ensuring that his weapon is in top condition and that he has trained himself to use it effectively?

The warrior knows what his weapon will do. He knows how to thrust and parry, how to hit the vital mark because he has made himself intimately familiar with his weapon's composition and capabilities. He has learned how to win the victory of righteousness with his weapon. And for the Christian, that weapon is the Word of God.

৵৽

---

[151] Philippians 1:12-13.
[152] Ephesians 6:17, RSV.
[153] Hebrews 4:12, NIV.
[154] 2 Corinthians 10:5, NIV.

"But I don't want to be called a 'Bible-thumper'! I don't think we ought to be bashing people with the Bible."

Listen, a warrior cannot be deluded by such enemy propaganda. We are not "bashing people with the Bible." But with God's Word as our all-powerful weapon of righteousness, we are going to take on all the ungodly ideas, arguments, pretensions and thoughts that stand against the Creator's holy, benevolent, and redemptive will. And with God's Word, we will not merely "thump" these things—we will demolish them.

And we will do this because the people who make these arguments and believe these ideas are not our enemies, they are spiritual captives, conscripted through the deceit of the devil and the sinful human inclination into the ranks of rebellion, serving the purpose of their own destruction.

With God's Word, we fight to free them from their sentence of current servitude and eternal condemnation. We wield the Word of God as our weapon, but the battle belongs to the Lord.[155]

❧

There are warriors among us today, men who have wielded the deadly weapons of war in the course of physical combat. We honor them, their sacrifices and their service.

But there are other warriors among us, too—warriors who have embraced the weapons of righteousness and stepped up into the ranks of the Christian soldiers engaged in spiritual warfare. The spiritual warrior does not grow old and tired and unfit for service as all who serve their country will. The spiritual warrior is not gender-restricted, for the battle against sin and evil rages in every heart and every relationship, in humble homes and the halls of great power.

❧

---

[155] Jamie Owens-Collins, "The Battle Belongs to the Lord," 1985 (from 1 Samuel 17:47).

On this Father's Day, it is right and appropriate to say, "Rise up, O Men of God,[156] Take up the shield of Faith. Take up the sword of God's Word."

If your shield is weak, then attend to it and strengthen it and draw it closer to you. If you do not know how to wield the sword God has issued you, then devote yourself to learning the skills that will help you master it, and train with those who can share their skills with you.

It is never too late, while you still breath the air of earth, to take up the weapons of righteousness and enlist in the service of your Lord.

But father or no—man or woman, young or old—spiritual warriors, rise up with the weapons of righteousness! Rise up, with faith and the Word! This world is engaged in spiritual warfare and every human being will serve on one side or the other. There is no neutrality or conscientious objection.

Rise up, spiritual warriors!

Rise up and serve your King!

৯৵৶

---

[156] William Pierson Merrill "Rise Up, O Men of God," 1911.

2 Corinthians 8:1-15 NRSV

¹ We want you to know, brothers and sisters, about the grace of God that has been granted to the churches of Macedonia; ² for during a severe ordeal of affliction, their abundant joy and their extreme poverty have overflowed in a wealth of generosity on their part. ³ For, as I can testify, they voluntarily gave according to their means, and even beyond their means, ⁴ begging us earnestly for the privilege of sharing in this ministry to the saints— ⁵ and this, not merely as we expected; they gave themselves first to the Lord and, by the will of God, to us, ⁶ so that we might urge Titus that, as he had already made a beginning, so he should also complete this generous undertaking among you. ⁷ Now as you excel in everything—in faith, in speech, in knowledge, in utmost eagerness, and in our love for you—so we want you to excel also in this generous undertaking.

⁸ I do not say this as a command, but I am testing the genuineness of your love against the earnestness of others. ⁹ For you know the generous act of our Lord Jesus Christ, that though he was rich, yet for your sakes he became poor, so that by his poverty you might become rich. ¹⁰ And in this matter I am giving my advice: it is appropriate for you who began last year not only to do something but even to desire to do something— ¹¹ now finish doing it, so that your eagerness may be matched by completing it according to your means. ¹² For if the eagerness is there, the gift is acceptable according to what one has—not according to what one does not have.

¹³ I do not mean that there should be relief for others and pressure on you, but it is a question of a fair balance between ¹⁴ your present abundance and their need, so that their abundance may be for your need, in order that there may be a fair balance.

¹⁵ As it is written,

> *"The one who had much did not have too much,*
> *and the one who had little did not have too little."*

⧽⧼

32.

The Generous Undertaking

2 Corinthians 8:1-15 NRSV

The sermon today was supposed to be my annual stewardship sermon. I'm supposed to preach one each year and I know you've been waiting eagerly for this one since the previous one last fall. I even had a pretty good three-point outline: "Give early. Give often. Give a lot."

But I picked the wrong scripture. I thought since Paul is telling a church to take up a collection in 2nd Corinthians 8 and 9, I could use what he says there to do the same thing with you. But the more I read, the more I realized: Paul isn't really talking about money— he doesn't even use the word. Paul is talking about grace.

కుండ

"We want you to know, brothers and sisters, about the grace of God that has been granted to the churches in Macedonia," Paul says. And he proceeds to tell them about it. And then, he reminds them that they already know what our Bibles call *"the generous act"* of our Lord Jesus Christ.

They know it because they believed the gospel when Paul shared it with them, and they experienced its impact for themselves in their salvation. But the word Paul actually uses for that *"generous act"* of the Lord Jesus Christ is *"grace."*

And when Paul says he wants them—their church—to excel in *"this generous undertaking"*—to complete the collection they began months earlier—again the word he uses is *"grace."*

"We want you to excel in 'this grace.'"

Everywhere you turn, there's grace.

You get the sense that more important than money—at least to Paul—and certainly to the churches up north in Macedonia—and hopefully to the church in Corinth—is grace.

So what's the big deal about grace? Or, in the words of a recent book: *What's So Amazing About Grace?* [157]

The dictionary defines "grace" as "unmerited divine assistance given humans for their regeneration or sanctification."[158]

That sounds a bit stuffy. Let me strip some of the chrome off it: Grace is something good that happens that you want or need very much, but that you can't get by yourself, or by waiting for it to happen naturally or accidentally, because it won't. Somebody else has to make grace happen for you—to you.

The ultimate example of this grace is the grace of our Lord Jesus Christ. The Christians in Corinth had received this grace. So have the Christians in this church and all the other churches around the world. Paul draws the picture this way: *"...though he was rich, yet for your sakes he became poor, so that by his poverty you might become rich."*

అ•ఆ

Now, I know he's talking about rich and poor, but Paul is still not talking about money. The Lord Jesus Christ was the kind of rich that owning everything in the universe and owing no taxes on

---

[157] Philip Yancey, *What's So Amazing About Grace?* Grand Rapids, MI: Zondervan, 1997.

[158] *Merriam-Webster Dictionary* (online) at https://www.merriam-webster.com/dictionary/grace.

it makes you. But He was richer than that because His wealth was not counted in physical things possessed because that was too insignificant to bother with compared with what else He was rich in.

You see, there are many different kinds of wealth, and the kind concerned with who can claim ownership of what on this one tiny planet for the few short years encompassed in a person's earthly existence is far down the line of importance in the ranking of types of wealth.

Far more valuable in God's eyes are things like wealth of ideas and wealth of energy, both of which played into Christ's role in creating the heavens and the earth and all that dwell therein.[159]

There is wealth of friends and family, like the unfathomably intimate and infinite relationship of the Father and the Son in the Godhead.[160] There is what Paul calls wealth of generosity, like what the Christ in heaven was willing to do for us,[161] which brings us back to this business of grace.

❧

When Paul says that the Lord was rich, he's referring to when the Lord was pre-existent in heaven, before He became human for all the Bethlehem-to-Calvary stuff.

What Paul does not mention, but the Christians in Corinth know to be true, is that while the Lord was infinitely rich in heaven, they and we were infinitely poor on earth. In fact, it turns out that you can be filthy rich in the things of earth and merely filthy in the eyes of God[162]—filthy and poor, as God measures it, needing grace.[163]

---

[159] John 1:1-3; Psalm 24:1.
[160] John 17:21; Colossians 1:19.
[161] Philippians 2:5-8.
[162] Revelation 3:17.
[163] Luke 16:19-26.

And to change our miserable condition—our spiritually impoverished condition—the Lord had to change His glorious, infinitely wealthy condition. He had to give it all up so that He could give us grace—that thing we needed and wanted but did not have, did not deserve and could not get for ourselves. He became poor—unimaginably poorer than He had been. And the sole purpose for His doing this was to make us rich in a wealth incomparably greater than the wealth of this world. Through His poverty, we became rich. Through His poverty, we got grace.

The song calls it "marvelous, infinite, matchless grace…grace that is greater than all my sin."[164] Grace, grace, God's grace….

Amazing!

ॐ

And then a funny thing happens.

A bunch of these churches north of Corinth—Philippi, Thessalonica and Berea probably—churches that Jesus has made rich in grace by His poverty—these churches want to become grace providers and not just grace receivers.

They're still poor as—well, church mice—in material wealth, but they realize they are rich in ways far more important. And they realize that by making themselves a little poorer materially, they can make others rich the way they are.

They realize that making others rich by their voluntary sacrifice of their material wealth, small as it is, makes them richer still—in grace—because they are doing for others what the Lord Jesus Christ did for them—not with *their* grace, of course, but with His.

You see, you cannot create grace, but you can channel it. Just as grace comes to you, undeserved, it can come *through you* to others. And so these poor church folks begged Paul for the opportunity to do what their Lord did, to become poor (or, in their

---

[164] Julia H. Johnston, "Grace Greater than Our Sin," 1911.

case, poor-er) materially, so that they could make other people richer, in material things—and, more importantly, in grace.

And in the process, by being allowed to participate in the grace-giving of Jesus, these givers of grace get even richer themselves—in grace. Their extreme physical poverty is no longer a show-stopper. Neither is the persecution their neighbors inflict on them. Their joy over what they are able to do for their Christian brothers and sisters is making them richer still—in generosity. They're making a spiritual "killing"!

And Paul writes to the church in Corinth about this new "growth market" in grace, and says, "You guys need to get in on this—you ought to get a piece of the action. You're richer than these other churches in material wealth. You're also rich in faith, in understanding and spreading the gospel, in your love for us.

"You need to get rich in grace by giving it to others, causing undeserved good to happen—causing people to encounter God who wouldn't—couldn't—of their own accord. And this time you can do it by giving other people some of the material wealth *you* don't need but they *do*."

God granted the Macedonian churches the treasure of the divine grace of salvation because He wanted them to have it—and then He granted them more grace because they *wanted* it—they wanted to be even richer in the kind of wealth that matters most—now and for all eternity. They wanted more grace—and they got it by copying the sacrificial love and commitment of the Lord Who gave them saving grace, first, and then, sustaining grace. Paul says, *"…they gave themselves first to the Lord."*

Everything else grew out of that.

⊱•⊰

The jury is out on the Corinthian church. The same grace our Lord gave the other churches—the other Christians—He gave to the church in Corinth. He has given them many more blessings than the other churches—or so it would seem to earthly eyes.

These Corinthian Christians are wealthy in many ways. But they have not yet made the full commitment of love that channels grace to others and returns additional grace for themselves.

And what about us?

Like the Corinthians, we are wealthy in many ways. We are wealthy in heritage and in talent. We are wealthy in commitment to worship, in zeal for God's Word and in the joy of our fellowship with one another. Some of us have been materially blessed to a greater degree than most.

But in one area of wealth—the most important—we are the same as all Christians: we are just as rich in grace as any other for whom our Lord divested Himself of all His divine assets and then gave up His life on earth.

So—"give early, give often, give a lot"?

How about: "Give yourself first and completely to the Lord Jesus Christ Who became poor to make you rich."

And then give yourself and the appropriate part of your resources to this generous undertaking—this grace—that channels God's grace to others and, in the process of your participation, multiplies God's grace to you?

We want you to know, brothers and sisters, about the grace of God that has been granted—to those churches—and to ours.

ॐ◌ॐ

Malachi 3:1, 3, 4 and 10 ESV

[1] *"Behold, I send my messenger, and he will prepare the way before me. And the Lord whom you seek will suddenly come to his temple; and the messenger of the covenant in whom you delight, behold, he is coming," says the* LORD *of hosts.*

[3] *"He will sit as a refiner and purifier of silver, and he will purify the sons of Levi and refine them like gold and silver, and they will bring offerings in righteousness to the* LORD. [4] *Then the offering of Judah and Jerusalem will be pleasing to the* LORD *as in the days of old and as in former years.*

[10] *"Bring the full tithe into the storehouse, that there may be food in my house. And thereby put me to the test," says the* LORD *of hosts, "if I will not open the windows of heaven for you and pour down for you a blessing until there is no more need."*

శ్రీ

2 Corinthians 9:6-15 ESV

⁶ *The point is this: whoever sows sparingly will also reap sparingly, and whoever sows bountifully will also reap bountifully.* ⁷ *Each one must give as he has decided in his heart, not reluctantly or under compulsion, for God loves a cheerful giver.* ⁸ *And God is able to make all grace abound to you, so that having all sufficiency in all things at all times, you may abound in every good work.* ⁹ *As it is written,*

> *"He has distributed freely,*
> *he has given to the poor;*
> *his righteousness endures forever."*

¹⁰ *He who supplies seed to the sower and bread for food will supply and multiply your seed for sowing and increase the harvest of your righteousness.* ¹¹ *You will be enriched in every way to be generous in every way, which through us will produce thanksgiving to God.* ¹² *For the ministry of this service is not only supplying the needs of the saints but is also overflowing in many thanksgivings to God.* ¹³ *By their approval of this service, they will glorify God because of your submission that comes from your confession of the gospel of Christ, and the generosity of your contribution for them and for all others,* ¹⁴ *while they long for you and pray for you, because of the surpassing grace of God upon you.* ¹⁵ *Thanks be to God for his inexpressible gift!*

ঌ৽ও

33.

Refined Gifts and Givers

Malachi 3:1, 3, 4 and 10; 2 Corinthians 9:6-15 ESV

Actions and attitudes. Of the two, we tend to focus on actions—what we *do*. God, Who is not indifferent to actions, seems more often more interested in attitudes—*why* we do what we do. If our actions need work, which they almost always do, God is more inclined to work on adjusting our attitudes than altering the offending actions, knowing (as God would) that our actions generally reflect and respond to our attitudes.

God says, *"Bring the whole tithe"* into His storehouse: an action. But Malachi doesn't say that God is going to come and haul us and our checkbooks into church and hover over us until we make the amount large enough to suit Him, and so fix an inadequate action.

No, God is going to come to us and refine and purify our attitude about stewardship so that what we think about it is in keeping with what *He* thinks about it, which will ensure that what we *do* about it is pleasing and acceptable in His sight.

Consider that image for a moment. Malachi says, *"the Lord you are seeking...and whom you desire is coming*—and when He does, He will refine and purify people just like someone would refine silver or gold."

Yikes!

And yet...how much better, more valuable and more wonderful is the purified version than the un-purified—of anything—including us?

What is God going to refine?

Not our actions, but our attitudes.

What does it mean for God to purify or refine an attitude?

It's an analogy, which allows for a little imaginative analysis. To be refined is to be put under some pressure that will so alter our natures that the impurities that have been so closely and tightly connected to our true essence will be dislodged and lose their hold on us. The more quickly we "let go" of those things that are not and should not be a part of us, the sooner the refining process will conclude (having achieved the desired result).

The goal of refining precious metals is to get to the pure state—to produce, for instance, pure gold. God's goal for refining His people is to produce attitudes that are as nearly "pure God" as possible. God's attitude is: "Nothing but the best for those I love." We saw that in Creation[165] and in His gift of His Son, Jesus Christ.[166] The attitude God is seeking in us as He refines us is the same: "Nothing but *my* best for the God Who loves me and gave Himself for me."[167]

God is refining and purifying so that selfishness is removed from the essential generosity of spirit with which we were created. God is refining out fear and distrust and cynicism so that faith and hope and love remain[168] as the motivating elements in our nature. God will work on these attitudes—*our* attitudes—until, as Malachi says, we present right offerings to the Lord—offerings pleasing to the Lord. The point is not the amount, but the motive—the attitude that wants to do what God wants us to do for the very same reasons God wants us to do it.

---

[165] Genesis 1:31.
[166] Matthew 3:17; 17:5.
[167] Galatians 2:20.
[168] 1 Corinthians 13:13, NIV.

Sometimes, we are refined and purified by pressure—hardship—the refiner's fire. And other times, we are refined in unexpectedly gentle ways. *"Test Me,"* God says, which really means: "Test your faith in Me. Suspend your uncertainties and your worldly (and, therefore, sinful) inclinations for a while and let Me show you how unfounded they are. Let Me win you over to a refined and holy attitude by divine generosity rather than hardship and adversity."

And yes, this turns what I was saying at the beginning about actions and attitudes on its head. But only temporarily.

God says, "Act, not in accordance with your attitude, but in direct contradiction to it, for a while—long enough for you to see what attitude is the purest and best for you. Let My response to your obedient actions show you the attitude you should adopt permanently to direct all your future actions. Let Me promote the proper attitude in you by showing you how I respond to proper actions. Let Me show you overwhelming blessings as though all of the goodness of heaven were falling on you."

❧

The cynic will say, "Why do I have to do what You want me to do before You will shower me with all Your blessings. Just shower me, already. Maybe my attitude will change."

Except that it won't, because God *has* been generous already. *"The steadfast love of the Lord never ceases; his mercies never come to an end."*[169] Even when your attitude is bad and your actions are worse, God is still good.

But this business of refining and purifying requires some form of engagement between God and the individual. This is an experiment in generosity. This is practical application of a divine truth. This is God's effort to get our hearts and minds where they need to be—not for God's sake, but for ours.

---

[169] Lamentations 3:22, RSV.

And so there must be some pressure—even if it is wonderfully positive—to move the mind and the heart of a man or woman in the right direction. We are the ones who will benefit from a refined and purified attitude, not God. *We* are why God bothers. God says, "Do what I have told you to do and see if it will not do wonders for you."

And if it does—and you see it and realize it—will not your attitude change—and all the subsequent actions that come from your purified perspective?

જ્જ

Paul picks up the same theme in 2nd Corinthians. Where Malachi was talking about fulfilling the old biblical requirements to support the religious structure—meeting the operating budget—Paul is writing his friends in Corinth about contributions they had volunteered to make to foreign missions and benevolence work. And he deals with their attitudes more than their actions.

"Each man should give what he has decided in his heart to give..." according to his attitude, *"not reluctantly or under compulsion...."* Here's the refining and purifying of the attitude of generosity, faith, hope and love, *"for God loves a cheerful giver...."*

Again, attitude—*how* you give—not actions—how *much* you give.

Paul acknowledges the practical benefit of their action: *"This service that you perform is...supplying the needs of God's people."*

But like God in Malachi, Paul is actually more interested in the refining, purifying benefit to the attitude that will *motivate* the action: *"Because of* [this]*...you have proved yourselves...."*

Your actions demonstrate your attitude.

And Paul points out that this refining of their attitudes will serve to further refine the attitudes of other people—the recipients of their gift: *"...men will praise God...for your generosity in sharing with them and with everyone else. And in their prayers for you their hearts will go out to you.... [Y]our generosity will result in thanksgiving to God."*

And if there is uncertainty on the Corinthians' part as to whether they should adopt the refined Christian attitude Paul promotes, he picks up Malachi's assurance of positive reinforcement: Act on the basis of God's call for generosity with your resources and see what God will do.

Paul says, *"God is able to make all grace abound to you, so that in all things at all times,* [you will have] *all that you need.... He...will...supply and increase your store of seed and will enlarge the harvest of your righteousness. You will be made rich in every way so that you can be generous on every occasion...."*

God refines both the giver and the gift: the attitude—and the action that results from it.

❧

Next week, we will celebrate our commitment to the ongoing ministries of our church. We will bring forward our pledges for the coming year in an act of sacrificial worship. But more important than the act is the attitude of generosity and faith each pledge will symbolize.

In the months ahead, we will also address ourselves to raising the funds to raise up a building for our church because, whatever we possess in the way of resources, we share the refinement of faith that God has worked in us, believing that God will make us able to provide a permanent place for His work in us and among us to continue.

God has been generous to us in pouring out His blessings abundantly upon us. And God has made us a generous people, from the day He brought our fellowship into existence, even until now. That attitude of gratitude and generosity, of confidence that He will enable us to be generous for Him like He has been to us, is one of God's greatest blessings in us. And He continues to refine it within us so that we may be pure in presenting our offerings to Him, offerings pleasing in His sight.

What we want to give God is His gift to us.
What we are able to give God is His gift to us as well.
Thanks be to God for these and all His gifts! Amen.

છે•જ્

Indices

Sermon Texts in Biblical Order

Sermon Texts in Biblical Order

Related Sermons in Other Volumes

Related Sermons in Other Volumes

Additional Scripture Passages Referenced

Additional Scripture Passages Referenced

Additional Scripture Passages Referenced

Sermon Texts in Lectionary Order

Sermon Texts in Lectionary Order

www.ingramcontent.com/pod-product-compliance
Lightning Source LLC
Chambersburg PA
CBHW020849090426
42736CB00008B/299